Congress and Public Policy

Lawrence C. Dodd
University of Texas at Austin

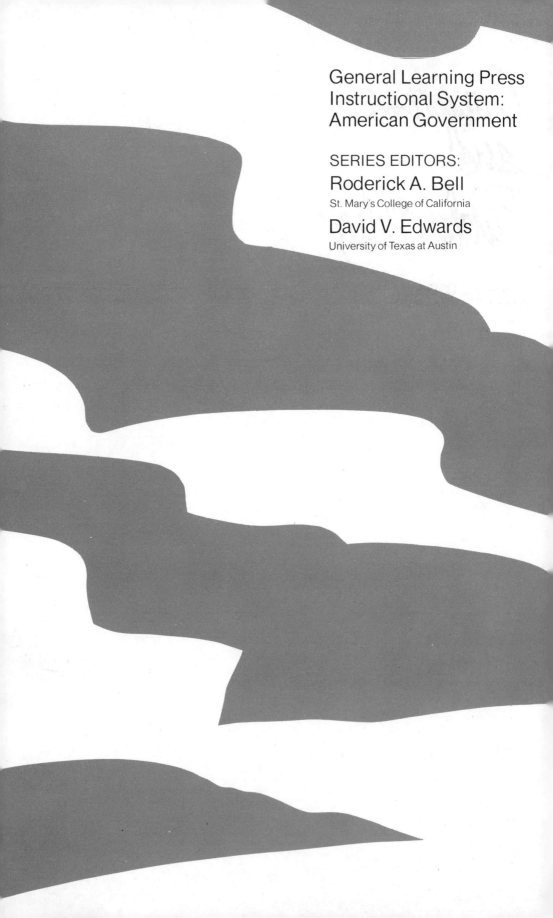

General Learning Press
Instructional System:
American Government

SERIES EDITORS:
Roderick A. Bell
St. Mary's College of California

David V. Edwards
University of Texas at Austin

Congress and Public Policy

Lawrence C. Dodd
University of Texas at Austin

GENERAL LEARNING PRESS
250 James Street
Morristown, New Jersey 07960

© 1975 Silver Burdett Company

Manufactured in the United States of America.

Published simultaneously in Canada.

Library of Congress Catalog Card Number 75-2947

ISBN: 0-382-18158-1

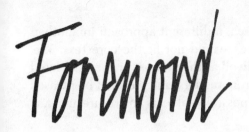

Foreword

This is one in a series of associated units that examine—in detail and from varying viewpoints—both traditional and newer areas of concern in American government and politics. *American Government: The Facts Reorganized,* the core text for this collection of materials on political science, is designed to unify the sprawling area of American government without sacrificing the facts and details that are normally to be found in a government text. This is accomplished by means of a powerful but simple organizational device: the "transformation paradigm." Essentially, the first half of the text presents and analyzes the checks-and-balances system of power distribution—its institutions and its politics—characteristic of pre-World War I America. The second half of the text presents a description and analysis of America as a modern administrative state, including the increasing concentration of power in the executive branch. The entire text is brief, concise, and, we hope, stimulating. These units are designed to complement the basic study we have written, and they may be combined with it in any fashion readers desire. But each unit is also an independent study on an important topic, and each can stand alone or be used to supplement other courses of study.

It is our hope that the basic text and these associated units will stimulate renewed interest in understanding American politics in the context both of its history and of its prospects. The core text packs basic facts into a concise analysis of American government, but the desirability of providing a more flexible course of study is obvious. The reader can use the associated units in this series to obtain further details in one area, a different approach in another, or treatment of a topic that just would not fit the core text. We, the authors of the core text, as well as the authors of the associated units, will welcome reactions from readers, and we shall be pleased also to receive suggestions of possible subjects for future units.

R.A.B.
Walnut Creek, California

D.V.E.
Austin, Texas

Preface

D—Yes, sir. I spent some years on the Hill myself and one of the things I always noted was the inability of the Congress to deal effectively with the Executive Branch because they have never provided themselves with adequate staffs, had adequate information available . . .

P—Well now they have huge staffs compared to what we had.

D—Well they have huge staffs, true, as opposed to what they had years ago. But they are still inadequate to deal effectively . . .

P—(Expletive deleted) Don't try to help them out.

*Presidential transcript of
conversation between John Dean
and Richard Nixon, Oval Office,
February 28, 1973*

Congress today is neither as impotent as many of its critics would argue, nor as strong as its proponents desire. Rather, it is in the twilight zone of American politics—too powerful to be ignored, yet too cumbersome to be fully effective. As a result, students often have a difficult time assessing Congress and its role in public policy. It is tempting to dismiss the legislature outright and focus on the president, but to do so is to vastly oversimplify American politics. To glorify Congress, on the other hand, as the embodiment of all that is positive and progressive in our society, is equally misleading.

The intent of this unit is to strike a balance between the simplified stereotypes, and to provide a realistic overview of Congress

Congress and Public Policy ☆ vii

as we enter the last quarter of the twentieth century. There are many intricacies of congressional organization, procedure, or behavior that are omitted here for lack of space. But rather than providing a simple enumeration of basic facts, the author tries to distinguish between congressional roles in policy formulation and policy surveillance, emphasizing the latter to an extent not often found in other discussions of Congress. While the unit provides a historical perspective on the national legislature and describes contemporary structure and procedure, the bulk of the discussion focuses on factors that aid or inhibit congressional activism and on reforms that might increase the chances for an autonomous, activist Congress. Among the more controversial of these reforms is one the author calls for: "responsible multipartism" in America.

It is my hope that this unit will be useful in any undergraduate course where students need a concise but systematic introduction to Congress. While avoiding extensive discussion, sufficient detail is provided to induce student interest in a variety of congressional areas. The bibliography is fairly comprehensive and should provide direction for students seeking to do further reading.

As the "Final Note" indicates, my own concern with Congress is in many ways a testament to my commitment to representative democracy. I see no way to sacrifice Congress and still maintain popular government in America. I am unwilling to forego popular, democratic government, however inadequate its current expression in our country may be. Thus I am concerned with understanding Congress and its shortcomings in the belief that through such understanding we can act more effectively to retain and improve our government. I hope the discussion contained in this unit may induce similar interests in its readers.

Lawrence C. Dodd

Contents

There is currently a great controversy surrounding the role of Congress in our political system and its impact on public policy. According to some scholars the influence of Congress has declined dramatically during the past two centuries. Thus Samuel Huntington, professor of government at Harvard, argues that "... the initiative in formulating legislation, in assigning legislative priorities, in arousing support for the legislation, and in determining the final content of the legislation enacted has clearly shifted to the executive branch" [1965, p. 23]. In the words of Roderick Bell and David Edwards, "This power has not been taken away [from Congress] by the Executive; it was *coopted*" [1974, p. 184]. Yet Congress does have its defenders. Ralph Huitt calls Congress "the durable partner" [1969]. In *Who Makes the Law?*, David Price states that Congress plays a vital role not only in "checking" the president and "refining" the president's proposals but in filling "policy gaps of its own and stimulating, cajoling, and assisting the executive to fill others" [1972, p. 332]. And, in a review of legislative action since 1940, Ronald C. Moe and Steven Teel write, "Our conclusion challenges the conventional wisdom that the president has come to enjoy an increasingly preponderant role in national policy-making.... Quite the contrary, the evidence suggests that Congress continues to be an active innovator and very much in the legislative business" [1971, p. 50].

Such conflicting views of Congress reflect differing interpretations of its role in two areas of public policy: policy formulation and policy surveillance. *Policy formulation* is the process by which are made the formal rules that are binding on society. This process includes the identification of societal problems that need governmental attention, initiation of proposals to resolve the problems, and deliberation and refinement of proposals. Further steps involve publicizing the problems and the alternative solutions, building a coalition behind the policy, drafting and submitting the bills to enact the policy, maneuvering the bills through Congress, and finally, legitimizing the policy by means of legislative approval. *Policy surveillance* is the process by which Congress investigates and regulates the implementation of public policy by the executive branch. Policy surveillance entails examining the effectiveness with which specific programs are enacted, the discretionary decisions made to see if they conform with the spirit and letter of the law, the organization of bureaucratic agencies to see if they are structured and run in a fashion that represents appropriate use of the people's money, the effect of a policy to see if it is the one desired.

Most political analysts agree that during the nineteenth century, while the congressional role in policy surveillance was minimal, Congress was paramount in policy formulation. Those who argue that Congress has declined maintain that (1) the role of Congress in policy formulation has been almost totally coopted by the president while (2) the shift of Congress to policy surveillance has been limited and haphazard. The defenders of Congress offer the alternative view that (1) the role of Congress in policy formulation has declined only slightly, the shift occurring principally in areas where Congress sets the original policy direction and leaves technical reformulations to the executive branch (under congressional surveillance), thereby allowing Congress to be innovative in policy areas not yet settled; (2) the role of Congress in policy surveillance has increased dramatically. The supporters of Congress believe that the current situation actually constitutes a congressional renaissance, with Congress today blending the roles of policy formulation and surveillance in a more effective and coordinated fashion.

The purpose of this unit is to specify changes in Congress since its establishment and to review some of the conditions that can affect congressional activism. The theme of the unit is that neither the congressional-decline model nor the congressional-renaissance model adequately characterize the effect of Congress on public policy during the twentieth century. Congress as an institution has not decayed but, in fact, has become increasingly capable of acting in an informed and deliberate manner. Despite structural and procedural changes that have strengthened its autonomy, however, Congress is not inherently activist. As is the case with most large, complex institutions, its structure and procedure are geared more to inaction than action, more to obstruction than speed; its actual role, whether active or passive, is a product of factors internal and external to Congress that can vary considerably from session to session. Reforms of Congress are possible that can improve its capacity to act; in the final analysis, however, Congress can do little more than that which its personnel and environment allow.

In the pages that follow, these arguments are developed in six parts. Part one reviews the changes that have occurred in the organization of Congress over the past two centuries, specifying in some detail the current structure of Congress. Part two indicates the formal and informal procedures that guide and constrain congressional action. Part three outlines some, though certainly not all, of the major factors that distinguish one Congress from another and that influence the degree of activism likely to characterize a given session of Congress. Part four presents a reappraisal of Congress distinct from both the congressional-decline and congressional-renaissance models. Part five outlines a series of possible reforms designed to strengthen the ability of Congress to play an active, autonomous role in policy formulation and policy surveillance. Part six concludes the arguments presented in the unit and reaffirms the author's commitment to popular government.

Congressional Organization

The United States Constitution established little formal basis for congressional organization and procedure. Aside from specifying that the vice president is the presiding officer of the Senate and that the Speaker of the House presides over that body, the Constitution left open most of the decisions in regard to congressional structure. Consequently, the organization and procedures of Congress have varied rather considerably over time. In discussing the role of Congress in our system, a first and central concern is whether the existing organization and procedures allow Congress to act in a well-informed, responsive, authoritative fashion. Do the patterns characterizing congressional deliberations aid or hinder a strong, autonomous, activist Congress; has Congress established a persistent, well-articulated, and coherent pattern of conducting its deliberations? It is a basic fact of congressional life today—just as it was one hundred years ago—that Congress is run by standing committees. The structure of the standing committee system has altered, the influence of party leadership has changed, the role of staff has increased; but through all of these and other changes, the influence of the committee system has remained dominant.

The Committee System Some periods of history are marked by efficient, coherent organization of congressional resources while others are characterized by structural chaos. The development of the committee system can be classified into four major eras [Polsby 1968; see also Cooper & Brady 1973; Galloway 1961; Morrow 1969; Ripley 1969b]. In the first era, dominated by Alexander Hamilton, the Congress did not use standing committees.

Some select (temporary) committees were employed for specialized service, but Congress primarily utilized a Committee of the Whole to conduct business. In the second stage of committee system development, characterized by presidential party dominance, President Thomas Jefferson and his party used committees to support presidential programs, publicize them, and maneuver them to congressional approval. The third period, symbolized by Henry Clay's rise to the House Speakership in 1811, witnessed the establishment of committees as strong congressional units of power, dominated by congressional leaders.

In the fourth period, called the decentralized stage, committees emerged as clearly autonomous units within Congress that were independent of presidential or party manipulation. The decentralized stage began in 1910 with the overthrow of Speaker Joe Cannon, who was stripped of his arbitrary power to determine the composition and leadership of committees. Until 1946 the committee system was characterized by autonomy from the executive and by internecine warfare within Congress. The 1946 Reorganization Act further decentralized the committee system. It fixed jurisdiction by rules so that each committee would have fairly clear areas of authority, although rules can never be so specific as to remove all ambiguity and conflict. The committee system is presently composed of two separate subsystems: the House committee system and the Senate committee system.

Tables 1 and 2 present the list of Senate and House committees for the Ninety-third Congress (1973–1974) and some relevant information about them. Column two presents the chairperson and ranking minority leader for the committee listed in column one. As committee leaders are immensely powerful individuals, column two of the table is a listing of many of the really powerful legislators in Congress. Column three indicates the size of the Democratic and Republican contingents on each committee, as well as the committee's total size. As can be seen, since the Democrats held a majority of the seats in both the House and the Senate during the Ninety-third Congress, they also held a majority of the seats on each congressional committee. It should also be noted that the committees in the House are generally much larger than those in the Senate; small House committees approximate the size of large Senate committees. In addition, a comparison of column three with column five will show that large committees often divide into numerous subcommittees. For example, the largest congressional committee (House Appropriations) divides into the largest number of subcommittees (thirteen). Often, it is in these subcommittees that committee work is actually conducted.

TABLE 1. Standing Committees in the Senate
Descriptive Characteristics for the 93rd Congress (1973–1974)

(1) Committee	(2) Leadership a. chairperson b. ranking minority member	(3) Size a. Democratic members b. Republican members c. Total	(4) Committee Preference Ordering (Prestige Rank)	(5) Number of Standing Committees	(6) Jurisdiction
Aeronautical and Space Sciences	a. Frank Moss (D-Utah) b. Barry Goldwater (R-Arizona)	a. 7 b. 6 c. 13	6	0	Aeronautical and space activities and related scientific matters, except those of a military nature.
Agriculture and Forestry	a. Herman Talmadge (D-Georgia) b. Carl Curtis (R-Nebraska)	a. 7 b. 6 c. 13	8	6	Agriculture in general, including farm credit and security, crop insurance, soil conservation and rural electrification; forestry in general.
Appropriations	a. John McClellan (D-Arkansas) b. Milton Young (R-North Dakota)	a. 15 b. 11 c. 26	2	13	Appropriations of government revenues.
Armed Services	a. John Stennis (D-Mississippi) b. Strom Thurmond (R-South Carolina)	a. 9 b. 6 c. 15	4	12	Military affairs, Panama Canal and Canal Zone, conservation of petroleum resources, strategic and critical materials; aeronautical and space activities peculiar to or primarily associated with development of weapons systems or military operations.

TABLE 1. Senate cont'd.

(1)	(2)	(3)	(4)	(5)	(6)
Banking, Housing and Urban Affairs	a. John Sparkman (D-Alabama) b. John Tower (R-Texas)	a. 9 b. 7 c. 16	11	7	Banking and currency generally; financial matters other than taxes and appropriations; public and private housing and economic controls; urban affairs.
Commerce	a. Warren Magnuson (D-Washington) b. Norris Cotton (R-New Hampshire)	a. 11 b. 7 c. 18	7	8	Regulation of interstate transportation, communications, inland waterways, Coast Guard, merchant marines, civil aeronautics except activities of National Aeronautics and Space Administration; fisheries and wildlife, Weather Bureau, Coast and Geodetic Survey, Bureau of Standards.
District of Columbia	a. Thomas Eagleton (D-Missouri) b. Charles Mathias, Jr. (R-Maryland)	a. 4 b. 3 c. 7	16	3	All measures relating to municipal affairs of the District of Columbia, except appropriations for its operations.
Finance	a. Russell Long (D-Louisiana) b. Wallace Bennett (R-Utah)	a. 10 b. 7 c. 17	3	6	Taxes, tariffs, import quotas, social security.
Foreign Relations	a. J. W. Fulbright (D-Arkansas) b. George Aiken (R-Vermont)	a. 10 b. 7 c. 17	1	10	Relations of United States with foreign nations generally; treaties; Red Cross, diplomatic service, United Nations, foreign loans.

Committee	Members			
Government Operations	a. Sam Ervin, Jr. (D-North Carolina) b. Charles Percy (R-Illinois)	a. 10 b. 6 c. 16	13	4	Budget and accounting measures; reorganization of the executive branch; general governmental relationships between the federal government and the states and municipalities, and between the United States and international organizations of which the United States is a member.
Interior and Insular Affairs	a. Henry Jackson (D-Washington) b. Paul Fannin (R-Arizona)	a. 7 b. 6 c. 13	10	7	Public lands, natural resources, territorial possessions of the United States, Indian affairs.
Judiciary	a. James Eastland (D-Mississippi) b. Roman Hruska (R-Nebraska)	a. 9 b. 7 c. 16	5	15	Federal courts and judges, civil rights, civil liberties, constitutional amendments, interstate compacts, immigration and naturalizaiton, apportionment of representatives, meetings of Congress and attendance of members, claims against the United States, Patent Office.
Labor and Public Welfare	a. Harrison Williams (D-New Jersey) b. Jacob Javits (R-New York)	a. 10 b. 6 c. 16	9	10	Education, labor, welfare, health, medical care.

TABLE 1. Senate cont'd.

(1)	(2)	(3)	(4)	(5)	(6)
Post Office and Civil Service	a. Gale McGee (D-Wyoming) b. Hiram Fong (R-Hawaii)	a. 5 b. 4 c. 9	15	3	Postal and federal civil services; census, National Archives.
Public Works	a. Jennings Randolph (D-West Virginia) b. Howard Baker (R-Tennessee)	a. 8 b. 6 c. 14	12	6	Public buildings, roads, flood control, rivers and harbors, stream pollution, water power.
Rules and Administration	a. Howard Cannon (D-Nevada) b. Marlow Cook (R-Kentucky)	a. 5 b. 4 c. 9	14	7	Senate administration generally; management of the Library of Congress, the Smithsonian Institution, etc.

TABLE 2. Standing Committees in the House of Representatives
Descriptive Characteristics for the 93rd Congress (1973–1974)

(1) Committee	(2) Leadership a. chairperson b. ranking minority member	(3) Size a. Democratic members b. Republican members c. Total	(4) Committee Preference Ordering (Prestige Rank)	(5) Number of Standing Committees	(6) Jurisdiction
Agriculture	a. W. R. Poage (D-Texas) b. Charles Teague (R-California)	a. 20 b. 16 c. 36	7	10	Agriculture and forestry in general; farm credit and security, crop insurance, soil conservation and rural electrification.
Appropriations	a. George Mahon (D-Texas) b. Elford Cederberg (R-Michigan)	a. 33 b. 22 c. 55	3	13	Appropriations of government revenues.
Armed Services	a. Edward Hebert (D-Louisiana) b. William Bray (R-Indiana)	a. 24 b. 19 c. 43	4	5	All matters relating to the national military establishment; conservation of petroleum resources; strategic and critical materials; scientific research and development in support of the armed services.
Banking and Currency	a. Wright Patman (D-Texas) b. William Widnall (R-New Jersey)	a. 24 b. 16 c. 40	11	8	Banking and currency generally; financial matters other than taxes and appropriations; public and private housing.

TABLE 2. House of Representatives cont'd.

(1)	(2)	(3)	(4)	(5)	(6)
District of Columbia	a. Charles Diggs (D-Michigan) b. Ancher Nelsen (R-Minnesota)	a. 14 b. 11 c. 25	15	6	All measures relating to municipal affairs of the District of Columbia except its appropriations.
Education and Welfare	a. Carl Perkins (D-Kentucky) b. Albert Quie (R-Minnesota)	a. 22 b. 16 c. 38	10	8	Education, labor, and welfare matters.
Foreign Affairs	a. Thomas Morgan (D-Pa.) b. William Mailliard (R-California)	a. 22 b. 18 c. 40	5	9	Relations of the United States with other nations and international organizations and movements.
Government Operations	a. Chet Holifield (D-California) b. Frank Horton (R-New Jersey)	a. 23 b. 18 c. 41	18	7	Budget and accounting measures; reorganization of the executive branch; intergovernmental relations.
House Administration	a. Wayne Hayes (D-Ohio) b. William Dickinson (R-Alabama)	b. 11 a. 15 c. 26	17	8	House administration generally; printing and correction of the *Congressional Record*; federal elections generally, management of the Library of Congress, supervision of the Smithsonian Institution.
Interior and Insular Affairs	a. James Haley (D-Florida) b. John Saylor (R-Pa.)	a. 23 b. 18 c. 41	14	7	Public lands, natural resources, territorial possessions of the United States, Indian affairs.

Committee	Members			Jurisdiction
Internal Security	a. Richard Ichord (D-Missouri) b. John Ashbrook (R-Ohio)	a. 5 b. 4 c. 9	13 0	Investigation of activities to determine if they are subversive.
Interstate and Foreign Commerce	a. Harley Staggers (D-West Virginia) b. Samuel Devine (R-Ohio)	a. 24 b. 19 c. 43	8 4	Regulation of interstate and foreign commerce and communications, regulations of interstate transmission of power (except between government projects), inland waterways, railroad labor, civil areonautics, Weather Bureau, securities and exchanges, interstate oil compacts, natural gas and public health.
Judiciary	a. Peter Rodino (D-New Jersey) b. Edward Hutchinson (R-Michigan)	a. 21 b. 17 c. 38	6 6	Judicial proceedings generally, impeachment proceedings, constitutional amendments, civil rights, civil liberties, interstate compacts, immigration and naturalization, apportionment of representatives, meetings of Congress and attendance of members, presidential succession.
Merchant Marine and Fisheries	a. Leonor Sullivan (D-Missouri) b. James Grover (R-New York)	a. 22 b. 17 c. 39	19 5	Merchant Marine generally, Coast Guard, Coast and Geodetic Survey, maintenance and operation of Panama Canal and administration of Canal Zone, fisheries and wildlife.

TABLE 2. House of Representatives cont'd.

(1)	(2)	(3)	(4)	(5)	(6)
Post Office and Civil Service	a. Thaddeus Dulski (D-New York) b. H. R. Gross (R-Iowa)	a. 15 b. 11 c. 26	16	6	Postal and federal civil services, census, National Archives.
Public Works	a. John Blatnik (D-Minnesota) b. William Harsha (R-Ohio)	a. 23 b. 16 c. 39	9	6	Public buildings and roads, flood control, improvement of rivers and harbors, water power, stream pollution.
Rules	a. Ray Madden (D-Indiana) b. Dave Martin (R-Nebraska)	a. 10 b. 5 c. 15	1	0	Rules and order of business in the House.
Science and Astronautics	a. Olin Teague (D-Texas) b. Charles Mosher (R-Ohio)	a. 17 b. 13 c. 30	12	6	Scientific and astronautical research and development generally, National Aeronautics and Space Administration, National Science Foundation, outer space, science scholarships, Bureau of Standards.
Veterans Affairs	a. W. J. B. Dorn (D-South Carolina) b. J. P. Hammerschmidt (R-Arkansas)	a. 15 b. 11 c. 26	20	5	Veterans' measures generally; pensions, armed forces life insurance, rehabilitation, education, medical care and treatment of veterans, veterans' hospitals.
Ways and Means	a. Wilbur Mills (D-Arkansas) b. Herman Schneebeli (R-Penn.)	a. 15 b. 10 c. 25	2	0	Revenue measures generally, tariffs and reciprocal trade agreement, Social Security.

NOTE: Information concerning committee preference ordering was derived from Morrow [1969, p. 42] and Rieselbach [1973, p. 60]. All other information comes from the 1973 *Congressional Quarterly Almanac*, pp. 1–17.

Column four indicates the relative prestige of the committees in each house based on the order of preference in which legislators sought assignments over the past several decades. It should be noted that there is a high degree of similarity between the prestigious committees of the two houses. In the Senate, the top five committees (in rank order) are Foreign Relations, Appropriations, Finance, Armed Services, and Judiciary. In the House, four committees among the top five have jurisdictions analogous to these five Senate committees; the four House committees with their prestige rankings are Foreign Relations (5), Appropriations (3), Ways and Means (analogous to Finance and number 2 in House), Armed Services (4). Only the House counterpart of the Senate Judiciary committee does not attain the top five. It is replaced by the Rules Committee, the most prestigious and one for which there is no Senate counterpart. It should be observed, however, that the House Judiciary Committee is the sixth most prestigious committee in that body. The similarity in the committee rankings between the two houses derives, in large part, from the similarity of authority inherent in the jurisdictions of the committees. These jurisdictions are enumerated in column six. A close examination of these jurisdictions is advisable for any student who seeks an understanding of the congressional committee system.

Today, the committee subsystems, in Nelson Polsby's term, are "institutionalized." Change is slow and, consequently, the information presented in table one will probably characterize the committees in each house for some time. The primary changes will come in committee leadership as legislators retire, die, or are defeated. When a legislator does leave Congress, thereby opening committee positions and possibly leadership positions, the committee positions he relinquishes are filled in a highly regularized fashion. For example, in the spring primaries of 1974, Chairman William Fulbright of the Senate Foreign Relations Committee was defeated in his bid for renomination by Governor Dale Bumpers of Arkansas. Fullbright vacated two different positions on the Senate Foreign Relations Committee: (a) his seat on the committee; (b) his position as chairman.

To fill a vacant seat such as Fulbright's on a committee, requests are taken from all members of the house who wish to fill the seat and who are members of the appropriate party. If only one legislator wants the seat, that individual normally receives it. If more than one individual wants the seat, however, the legislator with the most continuous *chamber* service (as a member of the appropriate party) usually receives the appointment, especially in the House of Representatives. Some discretion may be exercised based on the goals of the party leaders and the existing committee members. In addition, the leadership of the Democratic party in the Senate tries to ensure that all senators have at least one appointment to a major committee before any senator can serve on two major committees. But within these general parameters, house seniority is normally paramount when committee members are appointed.

Selection of a new chairman or ranking minority leader differs from selection of the new committee member. In Fulbright's case, for example, the senator receiving Fulbright's seat on the Foreign Relations Committee does not become the new chairperson. Rather, leadership of the Democratic party on the committee will go to the member of the committee who has the longest continuous service on the committee as a member of that party. In other words, party leadership on a committee is determined by *committee seniority*, not house seniority. Furthermore, committee seniority is a much more binding rule in the selection of committee leadership than is house seniority in the selection of committee members. So long as a legislator has the longest continuous service among his party members on a committee, he is virtually guaranteed his party's leadership position on that committee if he wants it. On the Foreign Relations Committee, for example, John Sparkman of Alabama is the individual with greatest committee seniority after the departure of Fulbright. Should Sparkman be willing to forego his chairmanship on the Senate Banking and Currency Committee in order to become chairman of the Foreign Relations Committee in the Ninety-fourth Congress, his selection as chairman should be automatic. A defeat of Sparkman (or even a serious challenge) would be an event of historic proportions.

The processes by which committee members and committee leaders are chosen attain significance because of the central role committees play in both policy formulation and policy surveillance. The committees have acquired the authority to hold hearings; to sit and act when and where they deem it advisable during sessions, recesses, and adjournment periods; to send for persons and papers that will aid them in deliberations; to take testimony on matters relating to policy formulation and policy surveillance [Morrow 1969, p. 16]. To be enacted, bills must be reviewed by the standing committees. In point of fact, most of the actual policy-formulation process within Congress occurs in committees. Once reported out of committee, most bills are largely assured of passage, though perhaps in amended form [Dodd 1972, p. 1136].

Although House and Senate committee systems are similar, there is a difference in the basic legislative focus and style of the two houses. Historically, because of the constitutional requirement that monetary bills originate in the House of Representatives, the House has emphasized financial legislation; similarly, because of the Constitution's requirement that the Senate give advice and consent to presidential appointments and to treaties that relate to international affairs, the Senate has tilted toward concern with foreign policy. In addition to these factors, as Richard Fenno points out, the Senate and House committee systems differ because "Senate and House committees operate in quite different institutional environments" [Fenno 1973, p. 145]. The Senate is smaller, more prestigious, and composed of individuals who by law serve longer terms than their House counterparts (six years in the Senate versus two years in the House). As a result, the Senate is more informal in its organization and procedure, and serious efforts are made to arrange meetings, debates, and votes to the advantage of all interested senators. Similar efforts are not possible in the House because of its larger size (435 versus the Senate's 100 members). In addition, since senators serve more heterogeneous constituencies (whole states rather than congressional districts), senators are normally interested in a wider range of policies and thus are more anxious to influence a wide range of legislation. The greater national prestige of senators, which gives them access to greater individual publicity, aids in this effort.

The result of all these factors is that senators tend to serve on more committees than do representatives: the smaller size of the Senate necessitates committee membership on two to four committees whereas in the House of Representatives the general norm is one committee assignment. As one senator remarked in an interview reported by Richard Fenno, "The House is a body of 435 struggling individuals whose only chance to have an impact is through their committees. The office of Senator is such, the prestige of office is such that a Senator can dabble in two or three areas that aren't necessarily in his committees. A House member can't do this" [1973, p. 147]. Consequently, while both Senate and House committees must make the final decisions on what legislation to report to the floor, influence of legislators in the Senate does not require membership on the key committee to the degree that similar influence in the House requires. Senate committee decision-making, in other words, is permeable: extra-committee senatorial influence is quite possible. On the other hand, House committee decision-making, especially on the major committees such as Appropriations and Ways and Means, is almost exclusively dominated by committee members.

These differences have critical implications for the style of the House and Senate in policy formulation and policy surveillance. The House is in essence a specialized, decentralized, hierarchically organized institution geared to the formulation of specific policies and to the surveillance of specific programs and agencies. By contrast, the Senate is a celebrated forum of debate, a stage for televised investigations into broad political problems such as the Vietnam War or Watergate, an arena from which individual spokesmen can identify and publicize critical national problems. The Senate is involved, therefore, in the formulation of broad policy perspectives and in building national policy coalitions. It informs the public as to the critical problems of the day and investigates indiscretions committed by the executive branch in its use of administrative authority. The House of Representatives on the other hand is involved in the detailed development of specific policy proposals, the aggregating of parochial interests, and the continuous oversight of specific agencies or programs. These contrasts should not be overdrawn, of course. Senators do formulate specific policies and investigate narrow questions of administrative action; representatives do at times initiate broad policy campaigns and conduct well-publicized surveillance activities. But generally, the actual roles of the two committee systems differ considerably.

This division of labor in the focus and style of legislative activity does cause problems. Senators tend to see representatives as narrow parochials concerned with only the specialized interests of homogeneous congressional districts, and as unconcerned with the broader questions of national interest. Representatives tend to see senators as dilettantes who talk a lot about a wide range of issues but know very little about any single issue. Thus the two houses often find themselves in heated institutional conflict, particularly when each passes legislation concerning a given problem and the legislation differs significantly in its content and implications. Such conflicts are especially possible since, as Sam Kernell has shown, in recent times, the Senate has been a more liberal chamber than the House "by a rather sizeable margin" [1973, p. 362; see also Froman 1963; Pressman 1966]. These differences are resolved—if they are resolved—in conference committees where members of each chamber meet together to draft a compromise bill that they hope will satisfy most of the members of both houses and pass the Congress. A recent study has shown that these conference committee decisions tend to favor the Senate's original position: "Senate influence in conference is found to greatly outweigh that of the House. Sixty-five percent of all conferences settled closer to the position of one chamber favored that of the Senate" [Vogler 1971, p. 110].

Despite the inherent conflict, the distinction between the House and the Senate committee systems can serve useful functions. It allows Congress to achieve the benefits of specialization, particularly in the House, without entirely losing the benefits that can accrue from legislators who are generalists. It allows Congress to play the role both of detailed policy surveillance and broad-gauge policy innovation. And it allows rather comprehensive and diversified review of legislation before passage.

The Congressional Party System Like the committee system, the party system in Congress has old roots but a modern form. In the House of Representatives the key party posts are the Speaker of the House, majority and minority leaders, party whips, and positions on the party committees, particularly the Committee on Committees. In the Senate the key party positions are majority and minority leaders, party whips, the party committees, and the president pro tempore of the Senate. Each of these has a historic tradition reaching deep into the American past; yet the role of each in the late twentieth century differs greatly from its role earlier in our history. Furthermore, the high degree of structure that characterizes the party system should not lead one to overestimate the party system's significance in Congress. The standing congressional committees are paramount, and individuals can gain significant power on committees with only nominal adherence to party. The structure of the party system will be outlined here; the influence of party in Congress will be discussed in a later section.

The Speaker of the House During the first decades of congressional history, "the Speakers were mere figureheads" [Galloway 1961, p. 97]. Then as today, the Speaker's position derived from the Constitution, and its occupant was nominally determined by vote of the whole House. Yet politics has always entered into selection. In the first several decades the Speaker was chosen by the ascendant faction, but they made their choice largely at the direction of the president. As George Galloway noted, the Speakership "was ... distinctly the gift of the President," particularly under Jefferson [1961, p. 98]. After Jefferson's presidency, Congress rebelled against executive control of the party leadership. A new group of dynamic young leaders took control of the House, among whom were Calhoun and Clay. They erected a party system based on the party caucus, and legislative leadership became the prerogative of individuals prominent in the House. In this new system, the Speaker became both presiding officer and leader of the majority party in the House. By 1825 the development of the committee system gave the Speaker his ultimate leverage: appointment of committee chairmen.

Throughout the nineteenth century, the power of the Speaker grew and consolidated. By the late nineteenth century, the Speaker had absolute discretion in the committee appointment process. Thus young Woodrow Wilson wrote in *Congressional Government:*

> The Speaker is expected to constitute the Committees in accordance with his own political views ... [and he] generally uses his powers as freely and imperatively as he is expected to use them. He unhesitatingly acts as the legislative chief of his party organizing the Committees in the interest of this or that policy, not covertly or on the sly, as one who does something of which he is ashamed, but openly and confidently, as one who does his duty ... [1885, pp. 85–86].

The arbitrary power of the Speaker is symbolized by Joseph Cannon (Speaker from 1903 until 1910). It was revolt against Cannon (1910) that brought a significant change in the Speakership and, indeed, in the entire power relations in the House. The revolt altered the Speaker's discretionary power in recognizing members, removed him as chairman of the Rules Committee (a position from which he had gained much power), and stripped him of his power to name committee members and chairmen.

Today, although the Speaker is formally elected by the entire House, in practice, he is selected by the majority party. He has normally served as floor leader of his party before moving into the Speakership. While seniority does not determine the Speakership, the last one hundred years has witnessed a dramatic increase in the number of years served by representatives before becoming Speaker. Today the Speaker has put in approximately thirty years prior service before becoming Speaker, while one hundred years ago the norm was ten years prior service in the House. At the beginning of the Ninety-third Congress, the Speaker was Democrat Carl Albert; before him the post was held by John McCormick and earlier by Sam Rayburn, both Democrats (reflecting the fact that the Democrats have controlled the House as well as the Senate since 1955).[1]

Floor Leaders and Party Committees in the House Aside from the Speaker, party leadership in the House rests with the majority and minority floor leaders and the respective party committees. The majority and minority floor leaders serve as chief party tactician and strategist on the House floor. Throughout the nineteenth century, the majority floor leader was selected by the Speaker. Since the 1910 revolt against Speaker Cannon, the majority floor leader has been selected by secret ballot in party caucus, as has the minority floor leader. The majority leader serves as the chief lieutenant of the Speaker in party business in the House; the minority leader is the minority party's prospective candidate for Speaker and its chief spokesman in the House. At the beginning of the Ninety-third Congress the majority leader in the House was Democrat "Tip" O'Neill. The majority leader, later to be vice president, and then president, was Republican Gerald Ford; he was followed by John Rhodes.

As in the case of the Speaker, the power of the floor leaders is largely informal. At their disposal are party whip organizations composed of a hierarchically arranged set of captains and subcaptains who "are (1) responsible for the pressure of their fellow party members, but . . . must also (2) transmit certain information to them, (3) ascertain how they will vote on selected important pieces of legislation, and (4) guide pressure to change the minds of the recalcitrant and stiffen the wills of the wavering" [Ripley 1964, pp. 561–576]. Given this network, the power of the floor leader depends upon his ability to develop, largely by means of persuasion, a cohesive party organization in the House.

---

1. For more extensive historical discussions of the speakership, see Nelson Polsby, "The Institutionalization of the House of Representatives" (1971, pp. 146–155); Randall B. Ripley, *Majority Party Leadership in Congress* (Little, Brown, 1969 a).

He does this by wielding influence on committee assignments, controlling information, trading favors, and logrolling.

Of course, any effective floor leader must have the support of the party's House committees (that is, those committees created by the individual parties to perform specific tasks). Each party's Committee on Committees is the most important of these. Established after 1910, these committees nominate members of the standing House committees, a power that has become tantamount to appointment since their nominees are invariably approved by the party caucuses. In the process of nomination, according to Nicholas Masters, the chief elements considered by these committees in their deliberations about general committee appointments, aside from house seniority, are (1) what assignments will further the reelection chances of the representatives; (2) does the geographical area that a legislator represents have a particular need for the committee representation; (3) does a particular legislator weaken or strengthen the ideological faction of the party with which the party leadership most identifies? In addition to these three considerations, if the committee is considered a "major" committee, a legislator must be perceived by the congressional leadership to be a "responsible" person, that is, a legislator likely to win reelection easily, and one who will maintain the committee's geographical balance [1970, pp. 46–67]. It goes without saying that these factors are open to considerable judgmental discretion—and therein lies the power of the Committee on Committees.

Aside from the Committee on Committees, each party in the House has a Congressional Campaign Committee. These committees arose during the period surrounding the impeachment of Andrew Johnson and were created to manage election campaigns. They are composed of one representative for each state that has a member in the House. Their basic functions are to supply limited financial assistance and service to party candidates in general elections. At times these committees appear to be tools by means of which the elected leadership in the House rewards representatives who "go along." Finally, each party in the House has a Policy Committee (formerly called steering committees). Formally, these committees are supposed to coordinate party strategy and tactics and to initiate policy innovations. As will be described later, this type of clear party coordination of policy positions has not emerged. The chairmen of these committees, as well as the occupants of other party leadership positions for the Ninety-third Congress, are listed in table 3.

TABLE 3. Congressional Party Leadership

Ninety-third Congress as of December, 1973

A. Democratic Leadership in Senate
    Floor leader—Mike Mansfield (Montana)
    President Pro Tempore—James O. Eastland (Mississippi)
    Whip—Robert C. Byrd (West Virginia)
    Assistant Whips—Ernest F. Hollings (South Carolina)
                Harold E. Hughes (Iowa)
                Daniel K. Inouye (Hawaii)
                Edmund S. Muskie (Maine)
    Chairman of the Party Conference—Mike Mansfield (Montana)
    Secretary of the Conference—Frank E. Moss (Utah)
    Policy Committee Chairman—Mike Mansfield (Montana)
    Legislative Review Committee Chairman—Edmund S. Muskie
    Steering Committee Chairman—Mike Mansfield
    Senatorial Campaign Committee Chairman—Ernest Hollings
            (South Carolina)

B. Republican Leadership in Senate
    Floor leader—Hugh Scott (Pennsylvania)
    Whip—Robert Griffin (Michigan)
    Assistant Whips—J. Glenn Beall, Jr. (Maryland)
                James Buckley (New York)
                William Roth, Jr. (Delaware)
                Ted Stevens (Alaska)
                Robert T. Stafford (Vermont)
                Robert Taft (Ohio)
                Lowell P. Weicker, Jr. (Connecticut)
    Chairman of the Party Conference—Norris Cotton
            (New Hampshire)
    Secretary of the Conference—Wallace F. Bennett (Utah)
    Policy Committee Chairman—John G. Tower (Texas)
    Committee on Committees Chairman—Jacob K. Javits (New York)
    Senatorial Campaign Committee Chairman—Bill Brock (Tennessee)

C. Democratic Leadership in House of Representatives
    Speaker—Carl Albert (Oklahoma)
    Floor leader—Thomas P. O'Neill, Jr. (Massachusetts)
    Whip—John J. McFall (California)
    Chief Deputy Whip—John Brademas (Indiana)
    Deputy Whips—Richard Fulton (Tennessee)
                Spark Matsunaga (Hawaii)
                Jim Wright (Texas)
    Assistant Whips—eighteen Representatives
    Chairman of the Caucus—Olin Teague (Texas)
    Secretary of the Caucus—Leonor Sullivan (Missouri)
    Committee on Committees Chairman (same as Ways and Means
            Committee)—Wilbur Mills (Arkansas)
    Democratic National Congressional Committee Chairman—
            Wayne Hayes (Ohio)
    Steering and Policy Committee Chairman—Carl Albert (Oklahoma)

D. Republican Leadership in House of Representatives
    Floor leader—John J. Rhodes (Arizona)
    Whip—Leslie Arends (Illinois)

TABLE 3. Congressional Party Leadership, Cont'd

Ninety-third Congress as of December, 1973

> Chairman of the Conference—John B. Anderson (Illinois)
> Vice Chairman of the Conference—Samuel Devine (Ohio)
> Secretary of the Conference—Jack Edwards (Alabama)
> Assistant Whips (Regional directors)—Albert Johnson
> (Pennsylvania)
> Samuel Devine (Ohio)
> Burt Talcott (California)
> There are 13 whips with special state designations
> Policy Committee Chairman—Barber Canable (New York)
> Committee on Committees Chairman—John Rhodes (Arizona)
> National Republican Congressional Committee Chairman—
> Robert Michels (Illinois)

NOTE: All leadership positions are based on the situation as of December, 1973. The source for this table is the 1973 *Congressional Quarterly Almanac* and the December, 1973 *Congressional Quarterly Weekly Review*.

The Senate Party System In the Senate, the most powerful party leaders are the floor leaders. Like the House, the Senate elects a presiding officer (the president pro tempore), but, unlike the Speaker of the House, the president pro tempore is not a powerful leader. Although he presides over the Senate in the absence of the vice president (a common situation), that function carries with it no significant power. Therefore, it is the Senate majority leader who is most comparable in party power to the Speaker of the House. The majority and minority leaders are elected by their party caucuses. As the chief spokesman of the majority party in the Senate, the majority leader is normally more powerful than the minority leader. This is not necessarily the case, however, if the Senate's minority party controls the presidency.

The emergence of majority and minority floor leaders is a post–Civil War phenomenon. Before the Civil War, as Randall Ripley has shown, there were "no easily identified floor leaders in the Senate and no formally elected party leaders. Individual Senators emerged as intellectual leaders or leading debaters only on specific issues. There were no party committees to help schedule the business of the Senate, take party positions or assign Senators to the Standing committees" [1969a, pp. 24–25]. During the Civil War, the Republican party began to develop as a strong force in the Senate. Periods of weakness alternated with periods of strength throughout the late nineteenth century, but slowly a tradition developed for the Republicans to elect a caucus chairman who was assured to be the party's floor leader. They created a Committee on Committees and developed a steering committee to help with scheduling. Similar patterns emerged among the postwar Democrats. By 1911 to 1913, the parties in the Senate had clearly established a practice of electing single majority and minority leaders "who would serve during an entire Congress and presumedly be reelected" [Ripley 1969b, p. 25]. Before this time, the real party leaders in the Senate were not necessarily the formal floor leaders or caucus chairmen; following 1911 to 1913, they were.

The Senate's floor leaders today "are, or have the potential for being, the principal forces in organizing the party, scheduling business for the Senate, promoting attendance on the floor, collecting and distributing information, persuading other Senators to vote with them on policy questions, and providing liaison with the White House" [Ripley 1969, p. 33]. The floor leaders have as part of their potential power resource the Senate party's whip system, but unlike the House, "in neither party are the whip and the floor leaders automatically like-minded colleagues able to work together effectively." According to Ripley, "at times a whip has come from a different faction within the party than the majority or minority leader. At other times, dissension has resulted from personal clashes between a whip and a floor leader" [1969, p. 35]. Overall, while the whips can help the floor leader perform his duties, their aid is generally peripheral and only a few have developed into major influences in their parties.

Aside from the floor leaders, party power resides with party committees. As in the House, each Senate party has its Committee on Committees and its Campaign Committee, each of which performs essentially the same functions as its counterpart in the House. The major difference in committee functions between the two houses is that the policy committees in the Senate are more important than in the House. Since the Senate Rules Committee does not have the scheduling power of the House Rules Committee, the majority party policy committee is the body of senators that the majority leader most directly and consistently consults in making his scheduling decisions.

In conclusion, contrasts between the House and the Senate party systems indicate that the House is much more hierarchical, decentralized, and formalized than the Senate. In the Senate the majority leader is much more a man among equals who gains his power almost entirely from his ability to blend the interests of his fellow senators with the interest of the party leadership. As a result, the nature of Senate party leadership is heavily dependent on the style and expertise of the majority leader. In terms of public policy, the House and Senate party systems are important first and foremost as communication networks that link the diverse individuals and committees in the two houses. Since the parties are not strongly programmatic, they do not themselves serve as the instigators of policy formulation or policy surveillance. But, in a Congress that otherwise would be centrifugal in its tendencies, the party system helps somewhat to bind together diverse interests and provide cues at the floor stage in legislative voting.

The Congressional Staff Along with the committee system and party system, the third important aspect of congressional organization is the staff. Pundits long familiar with Congress like to assert that "ours is government by the standing committee *staffs* of Congress." While this is an exaggeration, the existence of a well-developed legislative staff is crucial if Congress is to operate independently of the executive branch in the policy formulation and surveillance process. In a time of governmental complexity and extensive informational requirements, a well-developed congressional staff provides a source of independent investigatory and informational power for individual legislators as well as for the standing committees.

The congressional staff system, like the committee and party systems, is a phenomenon that has become institutionalized only very slowly over time. Kenneth Kofmehl reports that "prior to the middle of the nineteenth century, clerks were provided for congressional committees on a temporary basis by special resolution adopted by each house every session" [1962, p. 1]. Only in 1856 did two committees, the House Ways and Means Committee and the Senate Finance Committee, secure regular appropriations to pay full-time clerks. Not until the early 1900s did Congress regularly appropriate funds for the clerical staffs of standing committees and for the legislators themselves. The Legislative Reference Service and Office of Legislative Counsel, both sources of independent investigation and advice to legislators, were not created until 1914 and 1919 respectively [Kofmehl 1962, pp. 1–2].

The real emergence of the congressional staff came with the 1946 Legislative Reorganization Act. Before the 1946 act, as

Congressman Jerry Voorhis has noted, "the most minor bureau in the Department of Agriculture had on its staff a dozen people far more highly trained, far better informed, and considerably better paid than anyone on the staff of the Committee on Agriculture of the House or Senate" [Patterson 1970, p. 395]. The 1946 reorganization act authorized each committee to hire four professional aides and six clerks. Since then, as Samuel Patterson [1970, pp. 395–397] reports, "Committee staffs have grown fairly steadily in size. . . ." In 1947 House committees employed a total of about 222 persons; by 1955, approximately 350; by 1960, approximately 500; and by 1967, House committee staffs had grown to employ a total of 770 persons. Committee staffs have expanded similarly in the Senate: in 1952, the Senate committee staffs contained 340 persons; in 1967, the number was 620. A sizable proportion of this increase in committee staff members has been in professional (nonclerical) personnel. In the House the nonclerical staff increased from 51 in 1948 to 269 in 1967; in the Senate the increase was from 42 professional committee staff members in 1948 to 319 in 1967. As one would expect, this increase in committee staff members is reflected in significant increases in committee expenditures. Patterson shows that from 1955 to 1966, for example, congressional expenditures for staff inquiries and investigations doubled from 4.8 million dollars to 9.6 million [1970, p. 398]. Similar changes have occurred in the personal staffs for individual representatives and senators. In the short time period from 1967 to 1969, the number of representatives employing less than eight clerks declined from 113 to 44 while the number using ten or more rose from 184 to 265 [Tacheron & Udall 1970, p. 47].

The development of the congressional staff has thrust a new element—staff entrepreneurship—into policy formulation and surveillance. The creation of a professional staff both in the congressional committees and the legislator's personal office has led to a political substructure within Congress that can subtly maneuver representatives and senators into policy positions or surveillance activities that might not have been desired or taken without the pressure of staff (quite independent of the ability of staff to provide additional capacity for such actions). In fact, staff members from different offices have developed their own legislative caucuses and their own communication networks; the information and coordination made possible by these activities provide powerful mechanisms for staff influence in Congress, a factor augmented by the tendency of professional staff to make congressional service a lifetime career, thereby outlasting many legislators.[2]

Overall, the reliance of legislators on legislative staff is rather remarkable. Interviews with 160 members of the House of Representatives by John Saloma in 1965–1966 indicate a significant degree of conscious reliance by legislators on the staff in three areas of legislative behavior: legislative research; preparation for committee meetings and hearings; preparation for floor debates. Representatives rely most heavily on congressional staff for legislative research. In this area, the representatives report relying on staff 65 percent of the time, their own efforts 38 percent of the time, and on executive agency staffs 3.3 percent of the time. They reportedly rely on congressional staffs least in preparing for committee meetings and in preparing for floor debate. In these two areas, they rely on themselves approximately 60 percent of the time and congressional staff approximately 40 percent of the time. By their own admission, representatives today are highly dependent on congressional staffs [Tacheron & Udall 1970, pp. 303–311].

These findings are particularly interesting in light of more recent work by Norman Ornstein. According to Ornstein, reporting on a study of staffs in both the House and Senate from 1969 to 1974, the role of staffs in the Senate is even greater than the role in the House, particularly in the area of floor voting. In the House, scholars such as Matthews and Stimson [1970, 1975] have shown that representatives make many of their decisions by following "cues" of fellow representatives whom they respect. Yet in the Senate, Ornstein argues, "there is not the plethora of collegial sources present" that there are in the House. "There are no large state delegations, and the number and availability of committee 'cues' is more limited. Thus the potential of senators as information sources for their colleagues is considerably less than for representatives. And correspondingly, the role of Senate staffs is considerably larger" [Ornstein 1974b, p. 4].[3] Thus, when

---

2. The concept of staff entrepreneurship is suggested by David Price, *Who Makes the Law?* [1972]; see also John F. Manley, "Congressional Staff and Public Policy-Making: The Joint Committee on Internal Revenue Taxation," *Journal of Politics,* 30 (1968): 1046–1067; James D. Cochrane, "Partisan Aspects of Congressional Committee Staffing," *Western Political Quarterly,* XIV (1967): 381–389; Harrison W. Fox and Susan Webb Hammond, "Congressional Staffs and Congressional Change," paper prepared for delivery at the annual meeting of the American Political Science Association, New Orleans, Louisiana, September 4–8, 1973.

3. All quotations from papers by Norman Ornstein are reprinted with the permission of the author.

Ornstein asked senators how they obtained information to make voting decisions on the floor, they responded:

It is difficult. I have two bright young men on my legislative staff that try to keep me briefed as to what is coming up from time to time ... (Senior Southern Democrat)

I get it from my staff. I've got every committee covered by my legislative staff in addition to the committees I'm on. Every other committee has a person assigned to it or to a part of it. It is their responsibility to prepare me with the memoranda or information on the floor battle. To be here everyday and to have material on it. (Junior moderate Republican)

I depend more on my own staff than anything else. I have my legislative staff instructed to know at all times what is going on on the floor. They come up with 2 or 3 or 4 page memoranda on what the subjects are, pro and con, and how they think I probably should vote. I don't always go that way but at least I have a brief summary of what the matters are and the likely amendments and how they feel I should vote (Middle-seniority northern Democrat) [Ornstein 1974b, pp. 5–6].

These views contrast vividly with responses obtained from House members, emphasizing the greater Senate reliance on staff in the gathering of information:

On those bills on which I have doubts, I depend on friends whose views I can trust. Sometimes when I don't know the content of a bill or amendment, I look to see how others vote. (House member)

You get to know committee members and people who agree with you ideologically and go to them for information. Frequently, we go to the floor not knowing what bill or amendment is up, find out, then remember who is on the committee and talk to those with whom we agree (House member) [Stevens 1971, pp. 58–9; Ornstein 1974b, p. 5].

Based on interviews such as these, Ornstein concludes that 90 percent of the senators utilize staff resources in information gathering to a high extent, whereas only 20 percent of the representatives do. Aside from the fewer number of cues available to senators, the difference between staff utilization in the two houses is largely attributable to the greater overload of work senators face as compared to representatives: the smaller size of the Senate, combined with the large number of committees and subcommittees, means that senators are involved in a great deal more diverse activity than House members and, consequently, each senator has less time to spend in consultation with Senate colleagues on floor voting: the senator turns quite naturally to his personally chosen staff to guide his decisions rather than to colleagues who might provide conflicting cues.

Finally, the pattern of staff utilization is complicated further by differences within each house. According to Ornstein, in both the House and the Senate the average number of legislative staff personnel per legislator is greatest for northern Democrats, least for southern Democrats, with Republicans falling in the intermediate range. Within these party groupings, he finds that the more junior, ideologically liberal and urban-based members use more of their staff resources for legislative purposes. To explain these patterns, Ornstein concludes:

> In both the House and Senate, ideological liberals have more work cut out for them than their colleagues. Committed to social solutions which involve alterations of the existing governmental structure, they must formulate their ideas into legislation—this involves initial research and a subsequent translation into legal terminology. Moreover, and much more important, they are the most likely legislators to disagree with, to challenge, the legislative recommendations of the standing committees. With the vast, complex array of bills voted upon in House and Senate chambers, it is much less effort for legislators to cast ballots in accordance with the positions of the ranking members of the relevant committees. For one who is predisposed otherwise, additional information on the legislation is required before a vote can be cast—and, if a full-scale challenge is mounted, the legislators involved need additional resources, for information gathering and preparation of materials for debate, as well as for mounting collegial support for the effort [Ornstein 1974b, p. 3].

Congressional Procedures and Norms

The committee system and the party system provide the fundamental structure of Congress. They are separate yet interdependent organizations that crisscross one another to form an intricate maze. Undergirding this complex structure is the professional staff system of Congress. This staff system provides the essential labor force that allows the overall congressional structure to remain at least partially independent of the bureaucratic agencies and of the president. If Congress is organizationally a complex maze, the rules and norms that characterize the contemporary Congress function as a sophisticated map that guides the legislators, the lobbyists, the bureaucrats, and the interested observers through the maze.

The contemporary set of congressional rules and norms is a twentieth-century development, designed to meet twentieth-century needs. A complex organization requires complex formal and informal procedures to order the complexity and make it manageable; just as clearly, complex rules are unnecessary and undesirable in a simple organization dominated by the arbitrary rule of one or two individuals. Since the development of congressional organization and the development of congressional procedure occur in parallel, the history of one implies the history of the other. Therefore, I will forego extensive historical discussion of procedure in order to outline the existing rules and norms. For clarity and emphasis, the discussion is divided into three parts: (1) rules relating to policy formulation, (2) rules relating to policy surveillance, and (3) informal norms.

Formal Rules and Policy Formulation   The very nature of the congressional system, its tendency toward factionalism, its cross-cutting structures, make it essential that legislators have a set of rules by which to function. In terms of policy formulation, formal rules are critical because they outline the steps by which a bill becomes a law. The critical characteristic of these rules is that they create situations in which a well-placed minority can stop legislation that would be favored by a majority of Congress. Because the House is larger than the Senate, the rules are more complex and specific in the House, and legislation is more likely to be bottled up without reaching the floor. Nevertheless, formal rules are important factors in both bodies.

The most basic procedural fact about policy formulation is that before a bill can be voted on by all representatives or senators, it must be introduced by a single legislator or a small group of sponsoring legislators and referred to an appropriate committee; within committee it may be referred to a subcommittee. The committee or subcommittee will review a bill, modify or expand it, and then decide whether or not to report it to the entire house for consideration. A bill may stay at the committee stage from six months to the end of Congress (two years, if it was submitted early). It is only during a national crisis such as the energy shortage, or when legislation is inconsequential, that a bill will receive rapid review by a committee.[4]

While a bill is in committee, legislators or subcommittees specializing in the appropriate area will review it extensively. A bill can be killed within subcommittees or at the committee stage even though, were it voted on by the entire house, it might conceivably pass. Thus the first major hurdle is the subcommittee or committee, and its composition is critical. A conservative committee in a liberal Congress, for example, might kill legislation that otherwise would pass. The problem is compounded by the facts that bills must pass committees in both houses and that the authorization of a program and the appropriation of funds for a program are separate legislative items that must receive separate review. Any proposal requiring federal money is reviewed not only by the appropriate authorization committees but also by the House and Senate Appropriations Committees before it can become effective law.

The committee-subcommittee hurdle is fatal to most bills. In the Eighty-eighth Congress, for example, Lewis Froman [1967, p. 32] reports that 89 percent of all bills introduced in the House of Representatives were not reported by their committees to the floor of the House. Normally in such a situation, these bills are dead. Formal procedures can be used, however, in each house to bypass committees if they are delaying or killing bills. In the House, the major way to bypass committee is the *discharge rule*. According to the discharge rule, when a bill has been in a legislative committee for thirty days without having been reported, any member of the House can file a petition to have the bill considered for a House vote. If 218 members of the House sign the petition, then by a variety of technicalities a floor vote may eventually be achieved even though the committee continues to delay the bill.

The Senate has a similar rule; a majority vote is necessary to effect discharge. In addition, committees may be bypassed in

---

4. The following discussion draws heavily on Lewis Froman, *The Congressional Process: Strategies, Rules and Procedures* (Little, Brown, 1967); see also Floyd M. Riddick, *The United States Congress: Organization and Procedure* (Manassas, Virginia: National Capitol Publishers, 1949).

the Senate through the use of nongermane amendments, suspension of the rules, and by direct consideration of House-passed amendments. All of these procedures are quite difficult to use because of strong informal norms against interference in committee work, and they can be used effectively only with great strategic skill and only when a highly motivated legislative majority supports the bill [Froman 1967, pp. 90–95, 128–140].

The Rules Committee in the House (but not in the Senate) functions as an additional roadblock to floor votes on a bill. While some House bills are privileged and can go from committees directly to the House floor (general appropriations bills from the Appropriations Committee or revenue bills from Ways and Means are in this category), most bills, including virtually all bills of major consequence, must go to the committee on Rules before being considered on the floor. The Rules Committee gives the bill a rule stating the terms of floor debate. The rule determines such items as whether floor amendments to the bill will be allowed; that is, the committee establishes whether an open or a closed rule—closed meaning no amendments—shall prevail. While the Rules Committee normally cooperates and gives the bill's sponsor the rule he desires, there are times (particularly on critical bills) when the committee majority opposes the legislation and denies the entire House, which may favor the bill, a chance to review the bill. There are technical ways to bypass the Rules Committee, but they are seldom used and rarely successful [Froman 1967, pp. 52–61, 95–99].

Although there is no formal body in the Senate that can block a bill reported out by committee, in terms of delay and defeat, the Senate procedure most analogous in effect to the blocking action of the House Rules Committee is the *filibuster*. Once a Senate bill is reported out by a committee, it can go in a relatively direct manner (with some scheduling delays possible) to floor debate. But once a bill reaches the floor, the Senate has a sacred rule that a senator can speak for as long as he chooses. This rule is unique to the United States Senate among all the world's legislatures. Although debate in the House of Representatives is severely limited, in the Senate it may be interminable.

The tradition that senators may speak as long as they wish exists to protect minority rights. It is conceivable that without it, a minority might never succeed in presenting its view in a public forum. Seen in this light, the Senate's tradition of open debate is liberal in intent, a guarantee of free speech. On the other hand, if a minority that opposes a bill can manage to speak continuously for an indefinite period (filibuster) it may thwart the will of the majority by forcing the Senate to adjourn without voting on the bill. Thus, in an attempt to protect minority rights, the Senate faces the possibility of minority tyranny.

The only way a filibuster can be stopped is by a successful cloture petition (technically, by the invocation of Rule XXII). To implement cloture, sixteen senators must sign the petition calling for the closing of debate. The petition proposal is then brought to a vote and if two-thirds of those present and voting vote yea, the cloture motion passes. Once cloture passes, each senator may speak for *only* one hour on any amendment or bill already proposed. No additional amendments may be brought before the floor, and only germane amendments may be voted on. Within these limitations, the bill under consideration must come eventually to a vote.

If the procedure sounds simple, its simplicity is illusory. Since Senators of all ideological persuasions support the Senate's tradition of unhampered debate, it is extremely difficult to achieve the two-thirds majority necessary for cloture. In fact, it is quite possible for virtually every senator to support a bill that is being held up by a filibuster and yet refuse to vote for cloture because of reluctance to force an involuntary end to a colleague's speech. Consequently, from 1917, the year of the cloture rule's creation, to 1973, there were only seventy-nine cloture votes, of which fourteen were successful [*Congressional Quarterly Almanac* 1973, p. 30].

If a bill obtains a rule in the House and survives or avoids a filibuster in the Senate, still other formal procedures stand before it. While these are too numerous to specify all of them here, a few will suffice to illustrate the formal difficulty involved in lawmaking. Quorums must be maintained if the existence of a quorum is under challenge (in the Senate 51 members must be present and in the House 218); amendments that might gut a bill must be defeated; amendments that would make a bill unpassable or open to presidential veto must be avoided; motions to recommit the bill to committee must be defeated; the bill's supporters must be present and voting when it reaches the final vote. If a conference committee with the other house is required, the supporters of the bill must maneuver to sustain its provisions during conference and to achieve its final passage by both houses. Even if a bill survives all of these pitfalls, a presidential veto can kill it unless there is two-thirds vote in each house to override the veto.

Formal Rules and Policy Surveillance According to Emmette Redford in his study of the civil aviation activity during the Eighty-fifth Congress, "Congressional oversight of administrative agencies . . . is spotty, spasmodic and sometimes cursory" [1960, p. 225; see also Bibby 1963; Dimock 1929; Kerr 1963; Saloma 1969, pp. 130–168]. Much of the problem is due to the inadequacy of staff. Even though the congressional staff system has grown considerably over the past quarter of a century, most staff is devoted to matters of policy formulation or to congressional re-election efforts. Thus legislators and committees must rely for surveillance information on outside sources, particularly on the administrative agencies themselves. Furthermore, not only is lack of staff a problem but also policy surveillance is diffuse. There is no clearly established, easily observable, step-by-step process analogous to the process by which a bill becomes a law. Rather, there are numerous procedures by which committees examine, constrain, and guide administrative implementation of policy.

As Joseph Harris [1964, p. 8] has noted, "the predominant formal means of control is by the passage of statutes" that create and regulate the administrative agencies. Among the fundamental principles of our constitutional arrangement are the provisions that (1) executive agencies have only those powers granted to them by the legislature, (2) Congress can prescribe the internal organization of departments and agencies, (3) Congress can provide legislation regulating administrative personnel, (4) Congress can prescribe procedures of administrative action, and (5) Congress can appropriate administrative funds. Through all of these activities, as formalized in statutes, Congress has the basic responsibility for the creation and maintenance of agencies and their policy behavior. Since one form of control is abolition— or threat of abolition—Congress has in its statutory capability a powerful tool of surveillance.

Of these formal statutory controls, the appropriations process is the most significant. The basic means of control through appropriations is the ability to allocate funds to the major programs of each administrative department. Decisions to reduce spending for specific agencies can signal congressional displeasure with an offending agency by a surefire method. Because appropriations are the lifeblood of the agencies, reduction in funds, or threats of reduction, can produce significant alterations in agency policy. Consequently, agency personnel are quite receptive to the views and policy directives of the appropriations committees and sub-committees. Appropriations hearings become mini-investigations into agency efficiency, policy, and planning, with the appropriate subcommittees providing clear directives to agency personnel. Harris points out that the statutory power of appropriation implies also nonstatutory control by means of subcommittee directives.

> The hearings of the Appropriations subcommittees and their reports contain many examples of policy decisions and directives. Though policy decisions are often written into the Appropriations Acts, it is usually not necessary to do so since the subcommittees can issue verbal instructions to department officers, secure commitments from them as to future actions, or write policy directives in the reports, all of which actions have about the same effect as law. The questions asked of department witnesses during a hearing are strong indications of the subcommittee's wishes about policies and thus have an important effect on department administration and future plans. The determination of the amount of funds allocated to each program is in itself an important policy decision.[5]

Aside from statutory control and its nonstatutory by-products, formal powers of policy surveillance are exercised by congressional standing committees and select committees as *investigatory* bodies. Students in the age of Watergate are quite familiar with this phenomenon. Yet it was not until the Legislative Reorganization Act of 1946 that these congressional surveillance powers attained their current significance. The 1946 act gave clear statutory authority to each standing legislative committee to conduct investigations of the administration. Thus, while congressional investigations have existed since the earliest days of the Republic (the first occurred in spring of 1792 when the House of Representatives examined the defeat of the St. Clair expedition by Indian tribes in the Northwest Territory) only in the last quarter of a century have congressional investigations attained legitimate status as a function of the standing committees.

A third aspect of formal congressional surveillance power includes the Senate's constitutional power of advice and consent over many presidential nominations, which allows the Senate some influence on a president's selection of men. More often, it allows the Senate to elicit promises from presidential nominees

---

5. Reprinted with the permission of the publishers from Joseph P. Harris, *Congressional Control of Administration,* © 1964 by the Brookings Institution, Washington, D.C., p. 87.

concerning their behavior once in office. It was the power of advice and consent that led Attorney-general-designate Elliot Richardson to promise the creation of an independent special prosecutor of the Watergate affair who could not be removed except for gross misconduct. This promise later led to Richardson's resignation when, without having demonstrated gross, or, for that matter, any, misconduct on Archibald Cox's part, Richard Nixon ordered Richardson to dismiss Cox as special prosecutor. Thus, although the power to advise and consent is often exercised in a casual fashion, it can lead to dramatic confrontations between Congress, the president, and administrative officials.

Finally, formal congressional surveillance depends upon the "legislative veto." This form of control was first used in 1932 and has since become a significant surveillance technique. It requires that certain specific administrative decisions may be subjected to review for a specified time period by the two houses, a single house, or by a designated standing committee. The review period allows Congress the chance to "veto" executive action before it takes effect but after congressional authorization of the general program. This form of congressional surveillance is used to deal with problems of policy formulation and implementation in a complex age. In order to manage domestic problems such as economic crises or the energy shortage, Congress must often approve broad grants of authority so that the administration may take actions that cannot always be foreseen legislatively. Notwithstanding the delegation of broad powers, the congressional veto power allows Congress to constrain and guide the actual form of executive action [Harris 1964, pp. 204–248].

Informal Norms The House and Senate do not function solely along the lines prescribed by their formal rules. Indeed, informal norms or "folkways" are quite important in guiding congressional behavior and in sustaining a cordial, workmanlike atmosphere. Early in congressional history, for example, courtesy apparently was not an overriding concern among our legislators. Citations by Nelson Polsby [1968] of stories drawn from early congressional diaries and biographies depict a Congress that was much closer to the frontier mentality than is today's legislature.

Upon resuming his seat, after having replied to a severe personal arraignment of Henry Clay, former Speaker White, without the slightest warning, received a blow in the face. In the fight that followed a pistol was discharged wounding an officer of the police.

When Reuben M. Whitney was before a committee of investigation in 1837, Bailie Peyton, of Tennessee, taking offense at one of his answers, threatened him fiercely, and when he rose to claim the committee's protection, Mr. Peyton, with due and appropriate profanity, shouted: "You shan't say one word while you are in this room; if you do I will put you to death." The chairman, Henry A. Wise, added: "Yes; this insolence is insufferable." As both these gentlemen were armed with deadly weapons, the witness could hardly be blamed for not wanting to testify before the committee again.[6]

In 1851 in the Senate chambers Senator Charles Sumner was almost beaten to death by Representative Preston Brooks. "These were not pleasant days," Thomas B. Reed wrote; "Men were not nice in their treatment of each other" [Polsby 1968]. Such treatment contrasts vividly with a recent representative's remembrance of the postwar years. "One's overwhelming first impression as a member of Congress is the aura of friendliness that surrounds the life of a congressman. No wonder that 'few die and none resign.' Almost everyone is unfailingly polite and courteous. Window washer, clerks, senators—it cuts all ways. We live in a cocoon of good feeling" [Polsby 1968].

Along with the norm of courtesy, Donald Matthews [1960] reports in his study of the Senate of the mid-1950s that other norms exist. These include apprenticeship (being seen and not heard while learning the "system" in one's early days as a legislator); commitment to legislative work as the senator's basic duty; holding expertise as a basic value in one's legislative work; willingness to help other legislators (reciprocity) regardless of personal or ideological animosities; and institutional patriotism—an attachment to the Senate and to the legislative process as a means of conflict management. A recent study of the House of Representatives by Herbert Asher finds that analogous norms exist in varying degrees in the House. After interviewing a sample of nonfreshmen representatives, Asher concluded that the "highest level of agree-

---

6. Reprinted with the permission of the publishers from Nelson Polsby, "The Institutionalization of the House of Representatives," *American Political Science Review*, March 1968, 62: 166–167.

ment was reached on the importance of maintaining friendly relationships, with the importance of committee work running a close second, while the weakest consensus was found on the norm of apprenticeship" [1973, p. 501]. In Asher's study, only 38 percent of those interviewed maintained that freshmen should serve apprenticeships, while over 80 percent of the nonfreshmen representatives that he interviewed agreed that representatives should be specialists and should observe norms emphasizing legislative work, reciprocity, and courtesy. As to the low adherence to apprenticeship in the House as revealed by Asher's study (written in the early 1970s) versus the high level of adherence to apprenticeship reported by Matthew's study of the Senate (written in the middle and late 1950s), Asher concludes that "it is clear that the House (today) is not alone in its skepticism about apprenticeship; the norm of apprenticeship has fallen into bad times in the U.S. Senate as well, especially since 1964" [1973, p. 512].

Overall, the significance of these norms is that they increase the ability of individual legislators and of Congress as a whole to operate effectively. Were legislators in Congress consumed by interpersonal animosities and public conflict, little serious deliberation could take place. Without norms of work and specialization, representatives and senators would not be likely to develop the expertise necessary to draft legislation independently of the executive; nor would they be apt to investigate executive agencies and their implementation of policy. Reciprocity, however unwholesome it may appear to be in specific examples of "backscratching" and logrolling, allows legislators who possess diverse interests and knowledge to work together. Legislators are often quite parochial in their interests (few legislative acts have the full support of a clear Congressional majority), and the absence of reciprocity would probably consign Congress to permanent deadlock on many matters that appeal to special constituency interests. Institutional patriotism maintains the commitment to the legislative process that is necessary if legislators are to endure the hurdles that congressional structure and procedure throw in their way. It must be emphasized, however, that these norms are not always positive in their implications for congressional activism. For example, courtesy carried too far becomes an unwillingness to fight for principle against colleagues who might be intense in their feelings. Specialization often results in an unwillingness to listen to legislators who are not recognized experts in a field but who may nevertheless have useful perspectives on a topic. Institutional patriotism often blinds legislators to structural and procedural shortcomings whose removal might make Congress a more viable and active institution.

The Congressional Context

" 'You people have this congressional reform business all wrong,' a presidential press secretary once told a group of political scientists. 'What's wrong with Congress is not the rules, seniority, and all those things. What's wrong with Congress is the *people* in it. You're not going to change anything until you change that!' " [Price 1972, p. 11]. While this oversimplifies matters a bit, it is certainly true that congressional action or inaction is influenced just as much, if not more so, by the composition of Congress and the context within which the legislators work as by the organization and procedures of Congress.

When we evaluate Congress, we must realize that each Congress faces a different environment and that the role that Congress can play in policy formulation and surveillance is strongly influenced by events. A representative assembly is geared for deliberation, not speed. Thus, as Lawrence Chamberlain [1946] has shown, Congress tends to follow the president's lead in such immediate crises as war and depression but it tends to assert itself during periods of "normalcy." Therefore, before they reach a final conclusion, students who would evaluate Congress must take a close look at the factors aside from structural capacity that influence congressional activism.

Congressional Composition: The Ideology of Committee Leaders
Congressional style is just as dependent as presidential style is on the nature of the men who occupy the positions. James David Barber has shown that the behavior of the president depends on his personal characteristics.[7] Similarly, the activism of Congress depends on the characteristics of the men who are in Congress, particularly the men who chair the key committees, and on the precise composition of committees. It is rather shortsighted to

---

7. James David Barber, *The Presidential Character* (Prentice-Hall, 1972). For an earlier analysis of the impact of personality on state-legislature behavior, see James David Barber, *The Lawmakers* (Yale University Press, 1965).

complain that Congress as an institution is inactive or impotent if its inactivity is due not to inherent structural incapacity but to the nature of the men elected to office. If it is men and not institutions that cause the bottlenecks, it is men and not institutions that should be changed.

At the most basic level, of course, the composition of Congress is constant, at least in geographical terms. And even in terms of personnel, congressional turnover is quite low. As Nelson Polsby has shown, during the nation's first century, representatives in each Congress averaged approximately two years of prior service in the House; today the mean years of service has more than doubled to approximately five years [Polsby 1968, pp. 149–154; Cummings 1966]. Similar patterns obtain in the Senate: during the first century, senators for each Congress averaged around four years' prior service; today they average approximately ten years' prior service [Ripley 1969b, pp. 41–43]. Thus today, unlike a century ago, each Congress is composed mainly of members who have had a significant amount of prior congressional service. Legislators who try to return usually do return. As Warren Kostroski reports for the postwar years, ". . . United States senators have achieved re-election in more than 80 percent of their attempts . . . ; and congressmen have emerged victorious at a phenomenal 90 percent rate" [1973, p. 1213].

Despite low congressional turnover, committee membership does change considerably as legislators transfer from committee to committee [Bullock 1973, pp. 85–117; Fenno 1973, p. 112; Gawthorp 1966, pp. 366–373; Matthews 1960, pp. 148–152]. Composition varies a good bit from committee to committee in terms of such factors as geographical diversity, congressional seniority, committee member partisanship, and committee ideological persuasion [Fenno 1973]. And the pattern of personnel turnover that does occur from Congress to Congress can have significant effects at the committee level. For example, as noted earlier in this unit, a major determinant of power in Congress is committee seniority. In order to gain committee seniority, it is desirable to come from a state or congressional district that is relatively noncompetitive, a region dominated by one party. In an area of close party competition, the chances of being defeated are considerably higher, particularly during presidential election years, since presidential coattails can dramatically influence congressional races in marginal districts [Cummings 1966, pp. 1–27, 198–226]. Historically, the South has been the most persistent one-party region within the Democratic party, followed by the

West.[8] As a result, representatives and senators from the South have attained the greatest degree of consistent seniority, both in Congress as a whole and on the committees. As southern Democrats tend to be quite conservative ideologically, committee leadership has tended to be conservative in nature.

This fact has had a dramatic influence on congressional activism. Conservative committee chairmen, oriented toward the maintenance of the status quo, look hesitantly on broad, innovative efforts at policy formulation or surveillance [Donovan 1970; Price 1972]. Except in those rare times when conservatives are on the offensive seeking to repeal liberal social and economic legislation, conservative committee chairmen tend to maintain a low committee profile. Committee staffs are kept small, and subcommittees are given little support or autonomy [Goodwin 1970, p. 95]. To the degree that they are active, conservative committee chairmen, especially skillful ones, focus primarily on the surveillance of specific bureaucratic agencies and within the agencies on specific activities: are they inefficient or wasteful? Do they usurp congressional authority? Conservative committee chairmen are amenable to neither broad investigations into the desirability of new social and economic legislation nor to activist writing of innovative legislation. With conservative dominance of committees, the legislature is controlled by a set of individuals whose primary motivations favor a nonactivist Congress.

With the coming of the 1970s, the conservative dominance of committee leadership appears to be waning, although its departure is not complete, as a glance at the state designations of chairpersons in table 1 will indicate. As a general pattern, however, significant regional changes in party competition have occurred over the past quarter century. In 1947, 80 percent of the safe congressional seats within the Democratic party (that is, seats won by more than 65 percent of the general election votes) were southern congressional seats; by 1965 the southern share of the safe seats was down to 36 percent. The shift in safe seats has been to the northern, urban congressional districts. In 1946 northern urban congressional seats constituted 15 percent of the safe seats in the Democratic party. By 1965, the northern urban share approximated 50 percent. This shift is particularly significant since, over the time periods involved, the number of

---

8. For an extensive discussion and some necessary qualifications, see Barbara Hinckley, *The Seniority System in Congress* (Indiana University Press, 1971).

safe seats within the Democratic party increased from 110 (1947) to 142 (1955) to 166 (1965) [Wolfinger & Hollinger 1970].

With this shift in safe seats has come a shift in seniority. Today, the representatives and senators from outside the South maintain their seats most continuously and thus attain the greatest seniority. As a result, data prepared by Raye Lynne Macdonald shows that the leadership of the standing committees is shifting. This is especially true if we focus not simply on the attributes of committee chairpersons but rather on the attributes of the top three ranking members (including chairpersons) of each committee, so that we can estimate the direction of change over the coming decade, assuming that committee members ranking second and third in committee seniority will attain the chairpersonship within the decade. In 1951, as an average, 60 percent of the three most senior Democrats across all House committees were Southerners; in 1973 the analogous figures were only 35 percent. A similar pattern held for the Senate. In 1951 as an average, 57 percent of the three most senior Democratic senators across all committees were from the South, whereas in 1973, the figure was down to 31 percent. The increase in northern control of committees has come about primarily because of the rise in seniority of representatives and senators from northern urban constituencies. In the House of Representatives in 1951, northern urban representatives constituted only 32 percent of the top three members in seniority across all committees; by 1973, the figure was 52 percent. In the Senate in 1951, northern urban senators constituted only 9 percent of the top three in committee seniority for each committee; by 1973, they held 40 percent of the top three positions in committee seniority across all committees.

Estimates of congressional activism based on the intransigence of committee leadership during southern conservative dominance inaccurately portray the potential activism of a Congress newly dominated by northern urbanites. The potential for congressional activism in policy formulation is reflected in the passage of Great Society legislation, passage that many close observers of Congress maintain was due more to the shifts in congressional power than to President Lyndon Johnson's legislative skills. Since the Great Society days, congressional efforts to reform presidential campaign financing (stopped only by Richard Nixon's veto in 1971) and congressional limitations on presidential war-making powers symbolize continued activism. Similar changes are evident in policy surveillance. For example, George Shipley [1974] reports that House committee investigations more than doubled from 1947 to 1972. The increase occurred primarily in areas of broad-gauge investigations of programs; investigations of specific agencies actually declined over the time period.

The significance of this shift in congressional committee positions should not be overdrawn, however. It is always easier to obstruct than to innovate. A passive committee chairperson need only block activist measures, a procedure that can often be accomplished through the discretionary power of the chairperson without widespread committee support. By contrast, if an activist committee leader is to succeed, he or she must have the overt support of a majority of the committee. Thus, not only is the ideological persuasion of the chairperson important, but the composition of the entire committee is critical. The degree of committee cohesion or integration is one indicator of a committee's potential for activism.

Congressional Committee Composition: The Role of Integration
A committee is cohesive or integrated when there is a high degree of agreement on fundamental values or goals. When a committee is poorly integrated, it is characterized by high conflict between members, and few, if any, well-developed norms to regulate intra-committee behavior. Among the conditions conducive to committee integration, a first and major one is the intangible quality of committee leadership. For example, consider David Price's characterization of Senator Long as chairman of the Senate Finance Committee:

> The third factor militating against committee cohesiveness [of the Finance Committee] was the role of the *chairman*.... Long was personally flamboyant and temperamental; he was not an efficient organizer, nor was he particularly skilled at soothing animosity.... Rather than muting conflicts, he often intensified them. Unlike ... [Representative Wilbur] Mills, Long often became impatient with efforts to reach a consensus and attempted to work his will by means ill-designed to unify the Committee or to gain the trust of the parent chamber. Sometimes this meant using devious parliamentary tactics ... or giving covert support to opponents of a bill with which he had been entrusted.... On other occasions ... Long would push his colleagues to the limit ... [aiming] for the approval of the proposal that came closest

to what he wanted without great concern for the size of the margin.[9]

This contrasts vividly with John Manley's characterization of Chairman Wilbur Mills of the House Ways and Means Committee, Long's House counterpart, and "one of the most influential committee chairmen in recent years, if not in history."

> Mills' style of leadership, i.e., that he is a consensus-seeker, an observation made by almost everyone who has ever looked at the contemporary Committee, is of great interest. Mills' search for a consensus in the Committee is another way of saying that he is a democratic chairman of the Committee, a task leader who encourages the members to influence one another, who shares the quest for solutions to problems with the members ..., a leader who directs the members along lines he may favor but who does not attempt to force his predilections on others.
>
> To reach a consensus in the Committee Chairman Mills will compromise, bargain, cajole, swap, bend, plead, amend, coax and unite until as much of the controversy as possible is drained from the bill, and as many members of the Committee as possible support it.
>
> By stepping in at the right time and suggesting that a particular line of action may be acceptable to the members, and thereby resolving whatever tensions arise, he is seen by the members as "powerful," "smart," "expert," ... "pleasant," "patient," and the "peacemaker." ...[10]

As a consequence of Mills' leadership, the Ways and Means Committee is widely perceived as an integrated, cohesive committee; by contrast, under Long the Senate Finance Committee was quite unintegrated. Clearly, the personal style and skill of the committee chairperson can have significant influence on the integration of the committee.

Among other influences on committee integration, the stability of the committee membership is quite important. The more stable the membership, the greater the likelihood that, over time,

---

9. Reprinted with the permission of the publishers from David Price, *Who Makes the Law,* © 1972 by Schenkman Publishers, pp. 182–183.

10. Reprinted with the permission of the publishers of John F. Manley, "Wilbur Mills: A Study of Congressional Influence," *American Political Science Review,* 1969, 62:445.

the committee can develop a series of norms and working relationships among members that are conducive to at least some of the goals of most members [Fenno 1966, pp. 193–200; Price 1972, pp. 15–19]. The development of norms and common goals, of course, is affected also by the degree of similarity of committee members' constituencies. Committees composed of legislators with similar constituencies (especially as regards economic characteristics) tend to maintain greater committee integration than committees with dissimilar constituencies. This is almost surely due to the ideological similarity and the similarity of personal styles that characterize members from similar constituencies [Dodd 1972, p. 1141]. Still another contributing factor is the average seniority of committee members. Committees composed of a large proportion of senior, powerful legislators appear less integrated than committees composed primarily of less senior legislators. The apparent reason is that high congressional seniority reduces the necessity for committee members to conform to committee norms and goals as a source of legislative power [Dodd 1972, p. 1142]. All of these factors, as well as committee subject matter, the level of partisan division, and committee attractiveness can influence committee integration [Fenno 1966, pp. 193–200; Price 1972, pp. 15–18].

Committee integration is important for congressional activism because committees require some degree of agreement on values or goals before they can act in an effective and decisive manner. The type of action (or inaction) will depend on the motivational characteristics of committee members. David Price [1972] points out that a well-integrated committee may be just as passive as a poorly integrated committee if the integration centers on conservative, passive goals. However, some degree of integration would appear to be necessary if committees are to be activist. In other words, if the predominant orientation of a committee is activist, the success of the activist perspective will depend partially on the level of committee cohesiveness.

In policy formulation, committee integration is important in two primary ways. First, if committees are in fundamental disagreement internally, they will be unable to report legislation out of committee for consideration by the entire chamber. Thus the author's recent study [1972] of Senate committees during the Eighty-seventh Congress shows that among eleven basic programmatic committees, the success of committee members in achieving committee passage of their legislation was closely associated with the degree of integration that characterized the committee (as measured by an analysis of roll call vote cohesion). A second and related influence of committee integration is its impact on floor voting. Richard Fenno [1966, p. 501] in his study of the House Appropriations Committee states that "Of all the actions which promote success on the floor, the Committee takes the most important when it creates and maintains an internal structure for integrating its decision-making elements. Provided only that the context of its decisions does not constitute a gross violation of House ... expectations, Committee unity in defense of its recommendations is the necessary condition of victory on the floor."

While committee integration is useful in explaining variation in a specific committee's success over time it is not as important a factor in determining success across committees. Variation in floor success among committees depends upon many things, including that very potent element, the controversiality of the policy area [Dodd & Pierce 1975]. Nevertheless, it does seem quite plausible that for specific committees over time, success in achieving passage of legislation on the floor of the House or Senate is closely linked to the existence of moderate to high levels of committee cohesion.

Similar patterns exist in regard to policy surveillance. If committees or subcommittees are in fundamental disagreement on the appropriate focus of investigation, then in a world of limited resources, any surveillance activity will be stymied. Some degree of internal committee cohesion is a necessity if committees or subcommittees are to conduct broad-gauge, and effective investigations. In addition, committee integration would appear to be important for the success of surveillance activities once they are undertaken. For example, Fenno points out that a critical factor augmenting the influence of the House Appropriations Committee on executive agencies was the committee's ability to establish a stable relationship with the agencies.

> Both groups (the committee and the executive agencies) want to stabilize the relationship—want, that is, to keep conflict and uncertainty to a tolerable and predictable level—because it is in their interests to do so. . . .
>
> Such success as they have had heavily depends on the fact that mutual concerns plus repeated exposure to one another have given each a fairly accurate perception of the other. Each knows well how the other will, in fact, behave [1966, pp. 348–349].

This type of stable, mutually beneficial relationship is possible because the committee itself is stable and integrated in its internal activities.

Overall, it is difficult to state precisely to what degree integration has affected the increased role of Congress in policy formulation and policy surveillance. Very little work has been done by political analysts in this area. However, the increase in congressional policy formulation and surveillance noted earlier in these pages does coincide with an important change in Congress. In 1946 the Congressional Reorganization Act fundamentally restructured the committee system in both the House and Senate, reducing the former from forty-eight to nineteen (now twenty) committees and the latter from thirty-five to fifteen (now sixteen) committees. The result, it is fair to assume, was a rather severe blow to the integration of committees in the late 1940s and early 1950s. Almost surely, however, committee integration has increased over the last twenty-eight years as these new committees adjust to the new environment and as new systems or norms emerge. The inactivism of the late 1940s and 1950s in both policy formulation and surveillance may be at least in part a reflection of the low integration which was produced by the 1946 reform.

In conclusion, it would appear that the composition of congressional committees is critical as an influence on congressional activism. High committee integration and liberalism are conducive to congressional activism. Low integration and conservatism tend to encourage a passive Congress. Trends toward liberal domination of the committee system and increased committee integration over the past quarter of a century both herald an era of activism. However, certain qualifications of these statements are in order. First, it must be emphasized that the relationship between liberalism and activism is very much a phenomenon of our age. Liberal legislators have been, and apparently continue to be, the protagonists of the post–World War II world. But should liberal policymakers fully implement and fund their policies and thus become adherents of the status quo, or should they become disillusioned with their policies and flounder in confusion, then if reinvigorated conservatives can offer a coherent program of change, conservatism may become the force for congressional activism.

Second, to be effective, trends toward activism must penetrate not just one or two committees but the entire congressional system. Activism in any policy area requires an activist perspective in authorization committees in both houses, in the Appropriations subcommittees as well as the full Appropriations Committees, in the House Rules Committee, and of course, in each House as a voting body.

Third, despite the efforts of this unit to identify general patterns productive of committee activism, it must be noted that each committee is unique. Legislators seek and receive membership on different committees for very different reasons. Each committee exists in an environment of its own with its own special lobbyists, bureaucratic agencies, presidential pressures, and internal problems. As a result, the type of decisions taken, and indeed, the meaning of "activism" must ultimately be considered on a committee-by-committee basis. The ultimate generalization about the congressional committee system, as Fenno [1973, p. 280] reminds us, is that "congressional committees differ from one another. And House Committees differ from Senate Committees." Since committees differ, individuals wishing to influence specific committee decisions or to reform committees should ultimately choose a "selective strategy," one that recognizes the special qualities of the relevant committee(s). Some change in congressional activism can be effected by broad congressional reform. Ultimately, however, legislative activism in specific policy areas will require attention to the specific problems and environment of the committees concerned with the policy area.

Congressional Composition: Parties and Factions Whatever the nature of the congressional committee system, congressional activism is influenced by a number of other factors. Chief among these are the characteristics of the congressional party system. Students of American politics have long argued that an activist Congress requires cohesive, "responsible" parties, parties united around clear policy programs to which they are committed and which they will enact when in power. Just as firmly, American political analysts have argued that ideally there should be only two parties: a majority party that has the capacity to enact its policies without obstruction, and a minority party, that has the responsibility to act as the loyal opposition [American Political Science Association 1950]. The American congressional party system meets neither of these requirements. Rather, the parties— particularly the Democratic party—are broad coalitions of divergent groups united around the most general perception of public policy and historical tradition [Burns 1963]. It is no exaggeration to describe national party conventions more as quadrennial Donnybrooks than as love-fests. Bitterness over policy disputes often runs deeper among members of the same party than among members of different parties.

The primary policy distinction between Republicans and Democrats comes in the area of government management of the economy. As Aage Clausen has shown in his analysis of House and Senate roll call votes from 1953–1964, the two parties do have clear differences in this area:

> The policy dimension that most clearly separates Democrats from Republicans is the government management dimension. Indeed, the separation of the two parties is strikingly sharp; there is very, very little overlap on the policy positions of Democrats and Republicans. . . . On the dimension of government management it is very rare to find a Southern Democrat who is more conservative on the dimension than the most liberal Democrat.[11]

This difference should not be overstressed: though southern Democrats may be more activist in government management than Republicans, they may still be closer to the Republicans than to liberal Democrats. But, even allowing for divergent attitudes within each party, in government management, party does make a difference.

Since government management of the economy is one of the most persistent topics of our industrial age, the fact that the political parties divide over this topic, as well as over social welfare legislation and, to a degree, agricultural assistance means that party control of Congress can have significant implications. Republican control of Congress usually results in passive congressional posture toward economic regulation. In such a situation, any initiative in the direction of government control of the economy will come largely from the executive branch or from the minority party. Democratic control of Congress, even with conservative dominance, entails the possibility of an activist congressional orientation. The degree of potential activism will vary considerably, however, depending on whether conservative or liberal Democrats are the dominant congressional factions.

Outside of the economic area, the role of party as an activist influence is much less evident. In the area of civil liberties and

---

11. Reprinted with the permission of the publisher from Aage Clausen, *How Congressmen Decide* (St. Martin's Press, Inc., 1973, p. 114).

international intervention, the parties, particularly the Democratic party, are not united. In fact, as Clausen has noted, conflict over civil liberties cuts the Democratic party in half, with northern Democrats resembling Republicans more than they do southern Democrats [Clausen 1973, p. 114; Miller & Stokes 1963; pp. 45–57; Norpoth 1974]. In addition, at various times each party is split into isolationist and internationalist factions or, more recently, into "hawks" and "doves." As a consequence of these conflicts within the parties, congressional politics can be more accurately described as *multifactional politics* than as party politics, with Congress composed of at least four major factions: liberal Democrats, moderate Republicans, conservative Democrats and conservative Republicans. Liberal Democrats are characterized by a belief in high government activism in management of the economy, strong support for civil rights, and strong internationalism. Moderate Republicans differ from liberal Democrats primarily in greater hesitation about government management of the economy. Conservative Democrats evince a moderately activist stance on government management, but they oppose civil liberties legislation and tend toward isolationism in foreign affairs. Conservative Republicans differ from conservative Democrats primarily in their strong opposition to any government management of the economy and in greater openness to civil rights legislation.

Thus, far from the disciplined two-party system advocated by the American Political Science Association, these factions result in coalition politics within Congress. John Donovan [1970, pp. 61–62] has noted that "there are two bipartisan coalitions which ordinarily contend for power in Congress. The first coalition, composed of leading southern oligarchs and solid midwestern Republicans, forms the normal operational majority. The second coalition of liberal Democrats and a tiny band of moderate Republicans from the metropolitan areas form the minority legislative party, a minority which would support a liberal and activist president's domestic legislation." [12] Of the coalitions, the conservative group has the more extensive history. Formed in 1938 in reaction to Franklin D. Roosevelt's liberal, urban-oriented activism and particularly to his court-packing plan, the coalition has dominated the power positions of Congress for much of the past forty

---

12. From *The Policy Makers* by John C. Donovan, copyright © 1970 by The Western Publishing Company, Inc., reprinted by permission of The Bobbs-Merrill Company, Inc.

years. After achieving its height of legislative success during the 1950s the conservative group saw its dominance decline through most of the 1960s [Margolis 1972]. Much less a solid, institutional phenomenon, the heart of the liberal coalition is not a bipartisan alliance at all but rather the Democratic Study Group. Formed in the late 1950s in the House of Representatives, the Democratic Study Group is an organization of liberal Democrats that has provided a communications network and subcaucus for liberals in the House [Ferber 1971, pp. 249–269]. Lacking the power base and the cohesion that the conservatives have enjoyed, the activist-oriented liberals tend to fragment.

The persistence of multifactionalism in Congress is thus a long-term detriment to congressional activism. Even if the majority of Congress were activist, some way would have to be found to coordinate the efforts of the activists and offset the effects of those seniority differentials within parties that often hinder congressional activism; in other words, there must be some means to avoid or decrease obstruction of legislation by nonactivist legislators who obtain committee power through the operation of seniority despite their deviance from their party's less senior but activist majority. Disciplined parties offer one solution to this problem, yet such parties have not been forthcoming. Nor are they likely to emerge in the future out of the conservative and liberal coalitions, themselves "marriages of convenience" that include opposing factions. Civil rights is almost as divisive for the conservative coalition as it is for the Democratic party; government management of the economy is a persistent thorn in the side of the liberal coalition. Such fragmentation has produced a Congress that lacks mechanisms of coordination and order, and that is less activist in both policy formulation and policy surveillance than might otherwise be the case.

Presidents and Policies All of these patterns, of course, are affected by the nature of the president. When the president is of the same party or ideological persuasion as the majority party or ruling coalition in Congress, there is a tendency (often overemphasized in the literature) to rely on presidential leadership in policy formulation and to allow the president great discretion in policy implementation. By contrast, when the president and Congress differ in party or ideological persuasion, Congress will be more likely to assert itself. The implications of these patterns depend, of course, on the precise ideological tendency of Congress and the president.

When the president and Congress are both liberal, Congress will go along with activist programs supported by the president. In such situations, as Sundquist [1968] has emphasized, the president's program will in all probability be drawn from past proposals originated in Congress itself. As to policy surveillance, Congress will devote itself to broad policy questions, investigating the adequacy or inadequacy of policy programs but allowing the executive broad discretionary power in policy implementation. This was the situation that obtained during the Eighty-ninth Congress when Lyndon Johnson was president (1965–1966). The occurrence of a conservative Congress and a liberal president, illustrated by the Eighty-seventh Congress, which sat during John Kennedy's first two years as president, is characterized by congressional delay and amendment in policy formulation. In such a situation, if Congress is activist, it will normally be so in the area of policy surveillance, where it will investigate in narrowest detail the discretionary acts taken by the executive branch in policy implementation.

A conservative president together with a liberal Congress (particularly a veto-proof liberal majority) is a phenomenon that America has not fully experienced during the last forty years, though a sweep by liberal Democrats in the 1974 congressional elections could produce such a situation. The closest parallel is probably the relationship between the Ninety-third Congress (1973–1974) and Richard Nixon, though the activist element in Congress did not have a reliable, veto-proof majority. In the situation of a strong liberal congressional majority opposed by a conservative president, we would expect strong congressional activism in policy formulation, and numerous presidential vetoes. In policy surveillance, Congress would probably devote considerable attention to administrative oversight and control, investigating both the adequacy of existing policy programs and the appropriateness of discretionary administrative acts.

The final possible combination occurs when there is a conservative president and a conservative Congress. The Eisenhower years, particularly during the Eighty-third Congress (1953–1954), illustrate this situation. In such a condition, Congress will tend to support the president's passive stance in policy formulation. In policy surveillance, Congress will occupy itself with investigations into the narrow details of agency behavior, inefficiency, and waste.

Given the current trends of liberalism and conservatism in this country, the foregoing is probably a fair representation of congressional behavior under the specified combinations. However, as noted earlier, liberals could conceivably become protectors of the status quo at some point in the nation's future. Should this happen, conservative legislators—who have devoted their efforts to opposing liberal drives for expanded programs—could begin serious efforts at fundamental policy initiatives of their own, and the judgments presented above would reverse. If there are no changes in the relative activism of the differing ideological groupings, the combination productive of the most activist and autonomous Congress would appear to be a liberal Congress faced by a conservative president. A liberal Congress combined with a liberal president would produce a slightly less autonomous Congress, and so on.

Certain qualifications of these propositions are in order. First, much will depend on the margin existing within Congress between the ideological groupings and on the degree to which the majority ideological grouping has penetrated all committees, particularly the key committees, in both houses. Narrow majorities are unlikely to penetrate all committees and, if faced by a hostile president, will be unable to override presidential vetoes. Second, external events and external pressures are an important factor in legislative activism. As efforts by Common Cause and Nader's Raiders have shown, national pressure groups can mount significant campaigns for legislative action and can force legislators into activist positions that they would not otherwise take. The civil rights marches of the early 1960s were probably necessary preludes to the civil rights laws of 1964 and 1965. And Watergate, with the resultant weakening of the president's position, is almost surely an essential element in the congressional limitation of presidential war powers. Third, as has been noted, the ideological coalitions are not themselves cohesive entities. The conservative coalition will divide on some issues—notably civil rights—and the liberal coalition will divide on others. This, combined with the fact that presidential influence varies in Congress by policy area, means that congressional activism must be examined by policy area before reliable predictions about the probable success of any bill can be made.

Conclusion   The consideration of congressional activism in policy formulation and policy surveillance undertaken in this unit must, for reasons of space, neglect many facets. The basic point is that students interested in evaluating Congress should focus not just on the institutional matrix or on the momentary deadlock that may characterize any institution, but also on the behavorial and environmental context that critically affects congressional action. Among the factors influencing congressional behavior are the liberalism and integration of the committees, the cohesion of the parties, and the characteristics of the president. Yet even with these factors in mind, evaluations of Congress are tricky. Well-publicized efforts at social reform may be undertaken for superficial publicity while serious, long-term efforts by individuals or groups to bring about change may go unrecognized or, worse still, may be credited to an undeserving individual or group. This latter possibility is particularly important to keep in mind.

If you judge policy-making influence by determining merely whether the Congress or the president takes center stage in publicizing passage of a legislative program the president will almost invariably emerge the victor. The presidential State of the Union message, the traditional presentation of a formal legislative program made by modern presidents to Congress, the president's immediate access to national television and radio time, the fact that the president's signature on a bill is the last stage in the formulation process (thus the one easiest to publicize widely) and the president's ability to speak as a single individual while Congress speaks with many tongues, all enhance the president's symbolic quality as leader of legislation. Yet this symbol can be quite deluding. Where does the president's program come from? Who initially focused attention on the policy problem, publicized alternative solutions to the problem, formulated initial proposals? Who maneuvered the bill through Congress? Quite often the answers to these questions point not to the president but to Congress.

The most dramatic example of this confusion is the legislation of the Democratic party under John F. Kennedy and Lyndon Johnson. In the popular mind and in many academic treatises, this era represents the greatest period of presidential activism since Franklin Roosevelt's administration. The New Frontier and the Great Society have become symbols of the president's central role in policy making. Yet in reality, most of the legislation of this era originated with neither Kennedy nor Johnson. Rather, the program espoused and proclaimed by John Kennedy resulted from creative action taken in Congress throughout the 1950s. Sundquist [1968, p. 352] writes that "what emerges from a study of Democratic programs in the 1953–1960 period is a picture of block-by-block building under the leadership of those making up the activist triangle in the Senate, the House and the Democratic Advisory Council." This was the program later designated as the

New Frontier and the Great Society; its origin was almost entirely within the Congress.

Congress—Prospects for the Future

Throughout the past two centuries, Congress has undergone some fundamental transformations. With the creation of an autonomous committee system, Congress has become increasingly *decentralized.* Legislative authority is dispersed among twenty committees in the House and sixteen in the Senate. There is no single, powerful entity that provides clear, overarching coordination of the committees, even in the area of budgeting and finance. As a result, congressional activism is really a question of committee activism. In addition, Congress has become increasingly *professionalized.* Membership in Congress has taken on the characteristics of a profession, with individuals tending to view Congress as their central workplace and membership as a career. Senators and representatives are increasingly seeking and winning reelection, and they have at their disposal extensive services, particularly a sophisticated staff system. Finally, Congress has become an increasingly regulated institution. Explicit rules and implicit folkways have emerged over the past century that specify rather clearly the expected behavior of legislators. Norms such as seniority have developed that provide automatic procedures by which to make decisions that might otherwise prove explosive.

A Reappraisal   These changes have increased the Congress's potential for autonomy from the president by making the legislative branch more self-contained and self-sufficient. With the coming of a decentralized committee system in which membership and leadership are based on congressional rather than presidential considerations, Congress is *less,* not more, open to presidential co-optation: the president today is far less important in committee assignments than he was, for example, in the days of Thomas Jefferson. The increasing professionalization of congressmen means that they are today often as experienced, expert, and informed as the presidents or bureaucrats in specialized areas of public policy. And the increased internal regulation of congressional behavior means that much of the chaos and disorder, which often characterize (and obstruct) large institutions, are no longer prevalent in Congress, at least not to the extent that they were in the nineteenth century.

The significance of these alterations can be grasped best by comparing the United States Congress to legislatures in other countries. In such comparisons, the United States Congress invariably emerges as one of the most powerful legislatures in the world. Unlike Britain, for example, United States representatives and senators have

- their own offices and their own staffs
- well-developed committees to serve in drafting legislation and overseeing the executive
- significant financial resources to support their staffs and committee work
- a legislative party system at least partially independent of executive control
- well-developed and explicit procedural rules that protect and serve the interests of the individual legislator and the legislative leadership

Members of the British House of Commons, by contrast, have none of these, nor do members of most of the world's legislatures [Blondel 1973; Crick 1967; Shaw & Lees 1973; Sinclair 1974].

Nevertheless, the long-term changes in Congress have by no means ensured that it will be an activist legislature. On the one hand, as I have stated, congressional activism in both policy formulation and policy surveillance is dependent on such factors as the policy areas one is concerned with, the composition of Congress, the nature of the committee leadership, the integration of committees, the existence and nature of external crises, the ideological persuasion of the president, and his liberalism or conservatism relative to that of Congress. Typically, Congress will be less dominant and autonomous in periods of extreme crisis that require rapid action: in such situations it will allow the executive branch broad discretionary powers. But the fact that a specific Congress is quite passive or quite active does not mean that Congress as an institution is in permanent decline or is experiencing irreversible renaissance. By its very nature as a representative institution, the activism of Congress is going to vary considerably over time as its internal composition and external environment varies.

In addition, there are aspects of the current organization and procedure of Congress that hinder congressional activism. Each of the changes in Congress (decentralization, professionalization, increasing regulation) have shortcomings that hinder the ability of the legislature to act. Decentralization has not gone far enough; power has been dispersed only among a relatively small number of fairly autonomous individuals (the committee chairpersons). Such narrow dispersion of congressional power into the hands of a few autonomous individuals of great seniority (whatever their ideology) is not conducive to an activist Congress. On the one hand, coordination among committee leaders is largely absent, making the assumption of a coherent, activist policy role more difficult than it should be (thus the vices of decentralization are maintained). On the other hand, without widespread dispersal of power to less-senior members, incentives do not exist within a narrowly decentralized congressional structure for activism on the part of the younger members who might use it in an aggressive fashion. Such a denial of a "piece of the action" minimizes the chief virtue of decentralization—increased innovation from a wide spectrum of legislators.

The basic problem with professionalization is that it has not gone far enough, particularly in regard to the staff. First, there need to be clear standards and regulations for staff and hiring procedures. The rapid growth of staff that has occurred over the last quarter of a century allows the creation and appropriation of funds to positions that are often unnecessary and highly unregulated in usage. So a general review of staffing procedures should take place with greater emphasis on professional standards. Second, the increase in congressional staff that has occurred has been skewed toward the hiring of staff for the legislator's personal use and for activities geared to policy formulation, such as drafting legislation, and away from the hiring of staff of professional caliber for policy surveillance. Finally, staffs have often developed unevenly among committees because of differences in committee chairpersons. Many, if not most, committees could profitably employ more staff and technical resources.

Finally, in regard to the tendency toward increased regulation of internal congressional behavior, some of the procedures that have developed tend to make action by a congressional majority quite difficult. The most obvious of these, of course, is seniority. The reliance on the committee seniority rule to determine chairmanships among members of the majority party creates the possibility of individuals attaining congressional power who are quite unresponsive to the majority of their committee members, their parties, or Congress as a whole. As chairmen or chairwomen, such individuals can hinder and often effectively block efforts by the majority to formulate policy or conduct surveillance activities. In any case, whether the committee heads at a given time are representative or unrepresentative of Congress, they attain their offices in a quite arbitrary fashion, leaving congressional committee leadership selection to the whim of electoral accident and longevity rather than to the principle of congressional accountability.

Aside from seniority, the filibuster in the Senate and the Rules Committee in the House are the two greatest obstructions. The latter has been attacked repeatedly in past years by attempts to impose the Twenty-one Day Rule. All implementations of the Twenty-one Day Rule have been rescinded within only a few years of their enactment, though most activists agree that the Rules Committee should be stripped of its blocking power. The activists maintain that if the appropriate committees are willing to vote out a bill and both houses of Congress are willing to pass a bill, then the Rules Committee (which may be quite unrepresentative of Congress or the nation on a given question, and which has no specific expertise in most areas of legislation) should not have the power to block it. The position in relation to the filibuster, however, is a bit less clear. While the filibuster can be seriously misused, liberals and conservatives alike appreciate it as a protection against efforts to ramrod legislation down the throats of an intense minority that may need the rights to open debate to express symbolic opposition. Nevertheless, the filibuster does create severe problems when a minority stubbornly insists on obstructing majority efforts.

Reform Proposals To resolve the foregoing problems as well as others, students of Congress have suggested a number of reform proposals. According to Roger Davidson, David Kovenock and Michael O'Leary in *Congress in Crisis: Politics and Congressional Reform* [1969], there are three major models of reform that most writers advocate: the executive-force model, the responsible two-party system model, and the literary model. I will discuss the three paradigms and some of the major reforms they suggest, evaluating the adequacy of each as a base for strengthening Congress and making it more capable of activism in policy formulation and policy surveillance. Finally, I will suggest some reform proposals of my own.

The Executive-Force Model   First, Congress could be made formally subservient to the president. In order to avoid the problems inherent in a decentralized Congress, to provide legislative coordination, and to obtain a Congress that can act rapidly without procedural inadequacies, congressional structure and procedure could be altered to make it more compatible with presidential government. This position is shared by a fair number of political analysts and is often referred to as the executive-force model of American politics.

Supporters of this position advocate a number of reforms that are intended to increase the ability of the president to lead Congress by (1) his control of the congressional party and his influence (through the coattail effect) on congressional elections and (2) his control of broad grants of legislative power.. Among the changes recommended to augment presidential power are the strengthening of the national party organizations under the centralized leadership of the presidential nominees, the enactment of four-year terms for representatives that would coincide with presidential terms, and the unlimited reelection of the president. Reforms designed to increase the legislative power of the president would allow the president to veto any part of a bill (item veto) and reductions in the surveillance authority and capacity of Congress. In addition, all existing roadblocks to rapid legislative action, such as the filibuster and the House Rules Committee, would be abolished. In the long run, the executive-force model would result in the weakening of the entire committee system.

These reforms reflect the view that strong executive government is necessary and desirable and that strong congressional authority is undesirable and, indeed, counterproductive. Executive-force theorists assume that Congress by its very nature cannot be an effective independent policy formulater and, should it try to be, the result would be disastrous. Consequently, these theorists are willing to forego the attempt to sustain a strong, autonomous representative assembly in America. The basic trouble with this view is precisely that it removes from our political system a primary balance to the presidency. Under the executive-force model surveillance of the executive is largely nonexistent. Policy innovation that is independent of the executive branch is virtually impossible.

The Responsible Two-Party Model   A second perception of reform is held by those political analysts who see a responsible two-party system as the answer to congressional deadlock.[13] These theorists argue that the cause of congressional passivity and deadlock is the lack of cohesive, programmatic parties in Congress. What the country needs, according to this view, is a strong two-party system in which each party would take clear stands across all issues. The policy stance taken by a party in one region would be the same as the stance assumed by that party elsewhere. Voters across the country would thus share similar perceptions of the parties and could vote for parties with full knowledge of the policies they would enact once elected. Since this model envisions only two parties, elections would yield a majority party with a clear mandate to enact specific policies and a minority party with a clear mandate to oppose those policies by means of constant challenge and investigation. The majority party would control all committees and would provide coordination within the Congress.

In order to institute responsible two-party government, its advocates recommend a variety of reforms that would serve to create cohesive parties in Congress. These proposals include (1) national party clearance of local congressional candidates, (2) national party consent to the selection of congressional party leaders, and (3) the creation of party policy committees in Congress with power to discipline dissident legislators. Among the incentives that the party caucus would control are committee assignments, committee chairmanships, and financial support for legislators in congressional elections. Finally, to ensure the ability of the parties to govern, party reformers suggest strong party control of the House Rules Committee and abolition of the filibuster.

The responsible two-party government model of American politics is an extremely attractive one. Yet it falls apart in several places. First, and fundamentally, a legislative party system is at least as much a product of factors external to the legislature as it is a product of factors internal to the legislature. It is probably impossible to create a responsible *two*-party system in a country crisscrossed by such conflicts or cleavages as to make allies on one important issue become opponents on other important issues. A two-party system composed of cohesive parties requires simple lines of conflict that enable supporters of a given political party

---

13. American Political Science Association Committee, *Toward a Responsible Two-Party System* (1950). For an excellent survey of the positions associated with this model, see Eric M. Uslaner, "Conditions for Party Responsibility" (Ph.D. dissertation, University of Indiana, 1973).

to be in general agreement on all salient issues. If such agreement does not exist at the electoral level, if conflicts cut across one another, then cohesion is difficult, and a two-party system tends to fragment. In such a society, the party system must either contain a multiplicity of parties, or some large segment of the population must go unrepresented by parties. While the latter situation is opposed as undemocratic by most party theorists, the responsible multiparty system is opposed by two-party advocates because they mistrust the "coalition politics" that result when no party has a legislative majority. Thus responsible two-party theorists really face a dilemma: unless the structure of conflict in America changes (a change that cannot be brought about by reform legislation) responsible two-partism is impossible, however desirable it might be.

In addition, the two-party government model as articulated by most of its supporters could easily become a mechanism for executive dominance of Congress. The party government advocates seldom combine their call for responsible parties with other reforms that would strengthen congressional autonomy from the executive branch. They seem to be more concerned about reforms that would allow short-term social change through party government than they are about the long-term maintenance of balance between the executive and congressional branches. The extreme form of two-party government envisions a role of representation that is akin to automaton voting. There is little room in the ideal responsible two-party model for legislators who can serve as individual innovators of policy; and there is virtually no concern for the development of party-based mechanisms to advance congressional surveillance of the executive.

The Literary Model A third and final perspective on congressional reform that characterizes much of political analysis focuses on the establishment or perpetuation (depending on one's view of the current situation) of Congress as a governmental branch coequal with the executive. Advocates of this model view congressional constraints on the executive as a desirable and necessary element of democratic government in America. According to Davidson, Kovenock and O'Leary [1969, p. 17], "the literary theory is essentially a restatement of the constitutional formulation of blended and coordinated powers. . . . Adherence to this position need not imply a naive belief that nothing fundamental in the congressional environment has changed since 1789; it does imply, however, that the constitutional delineation of functions is still valid and that the relative weight assigned to the three branches is essentially correct." The great concern of the advocates of a literary interpretation of American politics is the maintenance or creation of a balance between Congress and the executive based on the original constitutional formulation of their respective powers and duties.

Supporters of this model suggest that the most essential reform is the repeal of the "reforms" of the last quarter century. First, the drive for equitable reapportionment of congressional districts based on the one-man one-vote principle should be rescinded; in its place, "legislative apportionment should recognize the validity of other criteria of representation—geographic interests, for example, or political subdivisions—in order to ensure that the greatest possible diversity of interests is embodied in Congress" [Davidson et al. 1969, p. 25]. This proposal goes hand in hand with others that would allow Congress authority over the actual electoral system employed. In addition, literary theorists oppose every move toward responsible parties, support maintenance of the Twenty-second Amendment limiting presidents to two terms, and oppose any other reform designed to impose an executive-force model on American politics. As to congressional procedures, literary theorists support the maintenance of the Senate filibuster, a strong House Rules Committee, the provision of increased staff for legislators and committees, and they oppose centralized congressional leadership.

These reforms are aimed at ensuring that Congresssional power shall balance presidential power and that Congress shall maintain its autonomy. They ensure that Congress shall represent a different constituency from that of the president, and that Congress cannot by presidential pressure be easily and rapidly forced to pass presidential legislation (thus the maintenance of the Senate filibuster and the House Rules Committee's power). The basic shortcoming of these reforms, from the standpoint of congressional activism, is that they make independent action by Congress in response to a congressional majority just as difficult as action by Congress in response to presidential pressure. In other words, the reforms would create an autonomous but dormant Congress capable of restraining the president but incapable of legislative action on its own.

Needless to say, the literary theory is supported primarily by conservatives who adhere to a very limited view of the proper role of government. The conservatism of its supporters is reflected in their support for a return to geographic or sectional representation rather than representation based on the one-man one-vote principle. The argument used to support geographic representation—that such representation would bring greater diversity into Congress—is fallacious on its face. It would, rather, hinder the representation of a large group of minorities now centered in the small geographic area of the nation's metropolitan centers. Were literary theorists really seeking greater diversity in Congress, they would support the implementation of a proportional representation system or a quota system, rather than the current plurality system.

What Is to Be Done?

A review of the major proposals for congressional reform reveals that none of them will produce a Congress that can protect its autonomy against presidential pressure and conduct simultaneously serious, sustained activity in policy formulation and surveillance. The executive-force model would produce a Congress dominated by the president in policy formulation and unable to check the executive through policy surveillance. The responsible two-party model provides reforms that simply will not work given the current complex of social cleavages in this country; if such a system were to work at all, it would almost inevitably tend toward executive-force politics. Finally, the literary model is inadequate: while it would seem to aid congressional autonomy, it does nothing to increase the possibility of congressional activism.

So what is to be done? Throughout this unit, I have emphasized that periods of congressional inactivity result not simply from the structure but also from the external environment and internal composition of Congress. As a result, reforms can never guarantee congressional activism, although some reforms are possible that would increase the possibilities for an activist Congress. I will discuss first, those changes geared to altering the party system and thus, to some extent, the external environment and internal composition; secondly, I will outline those changes that have as their goal the reform of the existing congressional structure.

Toward Responsible Multipartism   One obvious solution to many congressional problems is strong, cohesive parties. Were the parties in Congress committed to clear ideological objectives, were these views represented in a proportional fashion across all committees, and were the parties organized in a coherent fashion with clear lines of internal responsibility and communication, then the policy efforts of individuals on one committee could be linked directly with similar policy efforts on other committees, and party leadership would exist to augment and guide these programmatic efforts in both houses.

This situation does not exist within the United States Congress today because our two major parties are divided internally into factions that disagree intensely on certain areas of public policy. The conservative faction within the Democratic party often unites with the conservative faction in the Republican party against the moderate and liberal factions of each party. These conservative and liberal coalitions are not really surrogates for two responsible parties, however, since the coalitions are divided within themselves on certain critical policy areas. In fact, it is my suspicion that in a nation as diverse as ours, it is quite unlikely that it will ever be possible to maintain a responsible two-party system for any extensive period of time (although in an age of extreme economic depression, for example, we might experience short-term cohesion within two parties).

If we accept the view that responsible two-partism is probably untenable in this country, and if we still wish to obtain the benefits that responsible, cohesive parties could provide in Congress, I see no alternative to *responsible multipartism* (a situation in which there are three or more cohesive parties in the legislature, none of which controls a legislative majority). However, it is true that responsible multipartism may carry with it certain costs, for example,

1. Majority support for legislation requires coalition parties; the formation of such coalitions would necessitate extensive negotiations and compromises among the parties and might embroil the legislature in interparty intrigues that would not exist in responsible two-partism.

2. Such coalitions as actually form behind certain policy programs would often be undurable, and would thus provide no stable, authoritative policy perspective in the legislature.

3. With shifting party coalitions, it might be difficult for the

citizenry (or for the legislators themselves) to discern who is actually responsible for certain policy programs or for the failure of such programs. (It is more difficult to hold a party coalition accountable for policy success or failure than it is to hold a simple majority party accountable.)

4. Legislative multipartism does not mesh as well with a presidential-congressional system of government as does a responsible two-party system. Ideally a president should be elected by a partisan majority and should lead a cohesive majority party in Congress—yet multipartism presupposes that no majority party will exist.

Although multipartism has drawbacks, they are frequently overemphasized. Those problems that exist with regard to multipartism exist to an even greater degree with regard to multifactionalism, and multipartism has a number of advantages that make it more desirable than multifactionalism. In any case, it seems to me that since multipartism is becoming a distinct possibility in the United States, it behooves us to consider it as an alternative to the other reform proposals.

As to the penalties attached to responsible multipartism, while it is true that majorities require party coalitions and that the negotiations involved can be quite tedious, with intrigues abounding, multifactionalism presents the same problems. With multifactionalism the negotiating process is more difficult because of the lack or inadequacy of overt partisan organization, the diffuse nature of factional composition, and the lack of well-defined, legitimate factional leadership. Furthermore, faction members must withstand the constant cross-pressures that are exerted by their nominal party loyalties. By contrast, open, forthright multipartism could bring order and clarity to the coalition process. If the existing legislative factions were to attain the status of parties—with party leaders, party whips and staff, cohesive causes, and legitimacy in terms of congressional rules and procedures— negotiations in different policy areas would not only be easier within Congress, they would be more easily understood by the national citizenry. The current situation is quite confusing to the public when some Democrats and some Republicans vote for a bill against other Democrats and other Republicans: what party is to be held accountable for the bill or its defeat? Were the factions actually designated as parties, the lines of accountability would be much clearer, although still not as clear as in responsible two-partism, which in any case cannot exist in the American political climate. The key point is that responsible multipartism would increase the possibility of electoral accountability over the existing multifactionalism.

It is frequently said that multipartism generates undurable programmatic coalitions, but recent analysis of multipartism in a parliamentary context has shown that durable party coalitions can form in multiparty settings, and, in fact, are quite common. Transient coalitions form primarily in highly fractionalized settings (those with more than five or six parties) and in settings characterized by highly unstable parties [Dodd 1974, 1975]. The lines of factional cleavage in the United States would support probably no more than four to five significant congressional parties, were multipartism to arise at all (unless a highly proportional system of representation were instituted). In addition, our factional cleavages have been rather constant over time and should generate a stable multipartism, were other conditions to allow multiple parties. Thus the situation under which multipartism is most dangerous would probably not occur in our country. And, whatever the case in regard to the durability of multiparty coalitions, this argument against multipartism applies even more forcefully to factional coalitions. Within a coalition of responsible parties, party leaders can work closely with party membership to fulfill the bargains struck on specific compromises. Such efforts are much less possible with factions because factional leaders lack the legitimacy that party leaders enjoy and because factional leaders do not control the incentives that leaders of programmatic, cohesive parties can control. Stated quite simply, coalitions of factions are likely to be even more undurable and confusing than party coalitions.

The final response to the arguments that multipartism is untenable in a presidential-congressional system parallels the preceding argument. Multifactionalism produces the same problems in a presidential system as would multipartism, but without the benefits of multipartism. In contrast to responsible two-partism, multipartism would allow minority presidents, would create procedural difficulties in the selection of the president, and would increase the possibility that the president may be of one party while the Congress is controlled by a different party or coalition. But, the current situation also produces minority presidents. Of the twenty-seven men elected president since 1824, twelve (45 percent) won office at least once by less than a majority of the popular vote, including three of the last five (Harry Truman, John

Kennedy, and Richard Nixon). Properly instituted, multipartism could reduce the probability of similar occurrences in the future by limiting final presidential elections to slates receiving significant popular support on a first ballot vote, thus eliminating the marginal candidate. This process would negate the criticism that multipartism creates procedural problems in electing a president.

Procedural problems already exist in choosing our president. By maintaining the myth of two-partism, we allow a situation in which a narrow faction within each of the two parties can capture the nominating process and provide the nation with electoral choices that do not at all reflect dominant national sentiment. We need to face the unpleasant reality that existing multifactionalism within our nation requires an alteration in the current presidential selection procedures. Movement toward a multiparty system would permit us to establish a two-step electoral procedure in which a first election is held with all parties running a slate for president and vice president. Should a slate receive a majority of the popular vote, it would be elected. Otherwise, the slates receiving votes above a certain percentage (say 20 percent) could enter a runoff (with coalitions between slates possible in order to reach the qualifying limit). The slate with the largest plurality in the second election would win the presidency, and a minimum plurality required for victory could be specified (say 45 percent of the popular vote). If no candidate were to obtain this number of votes, the election could be thrown into the House of Representatives. All of this presupposes abolition of the Electoral College.

Two-step election procedures are not really outside of American electoral tradition. The procedure has been used in party primaries, for example. It would have the advantage of submitting to national popular vote a wider spectrum of choices, and of allowing the total national electorate to narrow the programmatic alternatives. And the procedural change at the presidential level would allow multipartism at the congressional level a greater chance of becoming institutionalized. It is true, of course, that one result could be a president and a vice president of one party (or of a coalition of two parties) and a Congress controlled by another. But similar results are already possible (and quite often occur) in the existing situation. For example, the Ninety-third Congress is dominated by the Democrats while the Republicans control the presidency. Change toward responsible multipartism might actually reduce the problem because the public would be more aware of the relationship between party label and programmatic stance of the candidates. No longer would a voter cast a ballot for a left-wing liberal and a right-wing conservative thinking that since both were Democrats, they both stood for the same policies.

As previously suggested multipartism could make the lines of congressional accountability clearer and result in an electorate more able to link responsibility for congressional action or inaction with specific parties and specific party coalitions. As the lines of congressional responsibility become clearer, the voters should be able to generate similar programmatic majorities at both the presidential and congressional levels. In addition, and critical to my position, responsible multipartism should make congressional activism increasingly possible.

In the current situation, the two parties are so disunited themselves that they provide only the most nominal coordination. The factions that form the basis for congressional behavior are not guaranteed representation on all committees and, in any case, they lack formalized leadership and procedural legitimacy. As a result, they cannot coordinate actions of their members across committees. In fact, their members may be distributed quite disproportionately and may not even sit on some committees that are central to the legislative process. Cohesive, well-organized parties that were represented proportionally across all committees and in each house of Congress could provide the necessary leadership, procedural legitimacy, and mechanisms for coordination of legislative activity.

As to decentralization, the key problem is that the current structure of congressional committees gives a significant degree of arbitrary power to a few autonomous senior legislators, while failing to disperse power sufficiently so that junior legislators can have access to the levers of power. Innovative legislators face potential obstruction from strong committee chairmen while all legislators lack the strong party organization with which to work for their policy views.

Multipartism could reduce this problem in several ways. The arbitrary, autonomous power of the current committee chairpersons stems from the lack of strong coordinating mechanisms in Congress. With cohesive parties, committee chairmen can be disciplined more readily by the parties, with leadership positions being distributed on the basis of adherence to party programs as well as seniority. At the same time, the parties would provide a mechanism by which junior legislators could make their innovative policy views known. In other words, within a well-institutionalized and strong committee system, responsible multipartism could provide a mechanism that would allow all legislators to propagate their policy views.

Another hindrance to congressional activism in the current Congress is the existence of rules and procedures that seriously inhibit the ability of legislators to act. A well-placed minority that has attained power through the operation of seniority, for example, can block legislation favored by a congressional majority. This problem has developed, at least in part, because legislators desire automatic procedures whereby to distribute power without becoming entangled in constant struggles. The lack of coherent policy perspectives within parties and the operation of seniority allow individuals to rise to power within a party who may be at odds politically with the party majority. To avoid this situation, we need to define more narrowly the boundaries of party membership in Congress so that a legislator who receives power through membership in a party generally represents the programmatic sentiment of that party. Multipartism does this.

Positions of congressional power under multipartism would be subject to negotiation among different parties. The organization of Congress would involve explicit recognition of policy differences among individuals and among parties. Such a situation would involve more open conflict early in a congressional session than now exists. On the other hand, it should reduce the long-term guerilla warfare that now takes place as legislators perpetually battle intransigent leadership that is chosen not because of policy perspective, but rather because of longevity. If a majority coalition of parties exists in Congress that can agree on certain policy perspectives (while disagreeing on others) such a coalition should be able to organize Congress and enact the general program.

Aside from its effects on coordination, decentralization, and internal regulation, a final and critical contribution of responsible multipartism is that it would not undermine an autonomous, powerful Congress. The goal of responsible two-partism is a cohesive majority party in Congress in league with a president of the same party; such a situation would almost surely reduce Congress to a stage on which policy programs developed elsewhere were announced and dutifully enacted. By contrast, the coalitional nature of multipartism would make the legislature itself a central arena within which policy negotiation would occur. In addition, multipartism can engender productive tensions in the legislature. One of the basic problems of responsible two-partism is that it would almost surely destroy the possibility of serious congressional surveillance of the executive branch. A majority party in Congress cannot easily investigate its own president as the symbolic lines of accountability would be too strong. By contrast, once the legislative majority becomes an explicit coalition of different parties, indiscretion by members of one coalitional party in the executive branch will not necessarily reflect directly or badly on the other coalitional party. In fact, the second party could well find disclosure of the indiscretion to its advantage. Such disclosure could discredit the first party while leaving its normal programmatic constituency open to advances of the second party.

All of these arguments, of course, suffer from a basic shortcoming. Responsible multipartism is not a reform easily enacted by altering a few laws, yet it may not only be desirable at this time but also possible. Increasing numbers of citizens are refusing to identify with either of the two major parties. In particular, there is a segment of the nation—the white Wallace voter of the South and elsewhere—that is disenchanted by the civil libertarian and welfare stances of the Democratic party, yet not compatible with the big business interests of the Republican party. The incentives that kept the congressional party leaders of the Wallace (formerly Dixiecrat) faction in the Democratic party (seniority and its rewards) are rapidly fading as the northern urban sections become the safe-seat districts of the party. Yet the Republican party does not provide the chance to recoup these incentives since the existing Republican party already has a well-established group of senior legislators. If the conservative Democrats are unsuccessful in their attempt to dominate the Democratic party (an attempt likely to face its full test in the 1976 presidential nominating process) then creation of a permanent third party is possible. On the other hand, should the conservatives dominate the Democratic party, it would surely drive the liberal Democrats to a third-party effort.

For a third party of either ideology (or both) to become institutionalized, the congressional incentive structure will need to be altered. Clear rules must be established for allocating seats on committees in rough proportion to a party's congressional strength; proportional procedures must be established for distributing staff and financial assistance among the parties and the party contingents on committees; formal procedures should be established to select a presiding officer, and perhaps certain assistants, so as to allow a set of organizational posts to be distributed among the parties in a congressional coalition. Finally, formal consideration should be given to new procedures for scheduling debates and votes when a clear majority does not exist —for example, a variant on the Rules Committee. Aside from these formal procedures, informal norms of interparty behavior would be necessary.

In addition to such changes within Congress—strange in their novelty but not impossible—institutionalization of multipartism would require some attention to new procedures for the selection of the president. The direction that such procedural changes might take were outlined earlier and would involve a two-step election process. These procedures would provide a system for the selection of the president that (1) was compatible with multipartism; (2) allowed popular rather than legislative selection of the chief executive, except in rare cases; (3) encouraged majoritarian presidents (although it did not guarantee them); and (4) allowed for an executive branch composed of party coalitions and that might include a president from one party, a vice president from another, and cabinet members from a range of parties. In many ways, of course, this is precisely what has happened in American politics in the past, but in a less overt fashion, with presidents such as Kennedy drawn from one faction and vice presidents such as Johnson from another.

My own suspicion is that if the rules governing congressional procedures and the presidential selection process were altered, institutionalization of third parties would be quite probable in American politics. I would expect a shrinkage of the Republican and Democratic parties to approximate 25 and 35 percent of the popular vote respectively in a normal first-stage election, accompanied by the growth of two smaller regional parties, one Southern in focus, one ultraliberal and northeastern in focus. All four parties would be relatively cohesive and form the basis of a rather persistent multipartism for the foreseeable future. This is not a prediction that such parties will definitely form but rather a recognition that conditions exist that could conceivably produce multipartism and that, if responsible multipartism should arise, it might conceivably be more beneficial than is the current multifactionalism masquerading as a two party system.

Other Structural Alterations The institutionalization of a multiparty system is one approach that conceivably could bring some necessary strength to Congress. But in many ways it is a "radical" step and one not easily legislated. Recognizing that the changes discussed above may be desirable, we must nevertheless turn attention to other reforms that can be considered in lieu of or in addition to the preceding ones. Assuming that our goal is an active, autonomous Congress and that to achieve this goal we must resolve problems relating to congressional coordination, decentralization, and internal regulation, several reforms seem desirable.

Greater coordination in Congress might be achieved by means of three basic changes. First, coordination between committees in the authorization and appropriation process might occur by allowing the new Budget Committee to set overall budgetary ceilings early in the year and to oversee the appropriation process in Congress. Such a system would allow individual authorization committees both to authorize policies and to vote the funds. In such a process, the voting of funds could take the form of specifying a percentage of the budget that would go to a specific policy area. The percentage would be a matter for negotiation between authorization committees and the Budget Committee. As Norman Ornstein [1974a, p. B-2] writes, "Combining the two functions (authorization and appropriations) and perhaps changing the budgetary process to a two-year or three-year cycle instead of the current annual go-around would likely bring about intelligent, and certainly more consistent, policy."

Secondly, increased use of joint committees between the House and the Senate would increase coordination between the two houses of Congress. As it is, the committee systems of the two houses largely mirror one another. There are some benefits from this situation, but the benefits accrue from the inherent differences between the Senate and the House rather than from differences in the committee systems themselves. Combining the committee systems would allow greater coordination while leaving untouched the distinction between the House and the Senate as autonomous voting bodies and as institutions that establish their own rules in terms of membership on committees. Such coordination of committees should also allow savings in terms of staff financing.

Also in need of coordination is policy surveillance. In this area one possibility for reform is the establishment of a full time Counsel for Legislative Oversight. Such a counsel would make available to different committees and subcommittees (1) a permanent expert staff trained in the rules, procedures, and informal norms of policy and agency investigation; (2) a clearinghouse for information concerning investigations by other committees; and (3) ready access to the conclusions reached on the basis of such investigations. While the creation of such a counsel, together with greater use of joint committees and a Budget Committee, will not resolve all problems of coordination, they are structural changes that should increase the possibility of coordination. And they are changes that should be relevant equally to the current party setting and to a multiparty setting.

The problem with decentralization in the Congress, as argued earlier in this unit, is that the decentralization that exists does not go far enough. One reform intended to improve the distribution of power while maintaining autonomous committees has already been undertaken in recent years. As a result of liberal efforts, Democrats in Congress determined in 1971 that when their party controls the House of Representatives, subcommittee chairmanships will be limited to one per party member; subcommittees are now to be permitted a professional staff; they now will have fixed jurisdictions, the power to handle legislation on the House floor, and a formalized procedure for the selection of subcommittee chairmen. These reforms serve to spread out power in the House. As Ornstein [1973, pp. 11–12, 17] has concluded, the changes have "brought in a minimum of sixteen new subcommittee chairmen" from 1971 to 1973; "spread power to younger, less senior members"; "improved the lot of non-Southern and liberal Democrats"; and, in the long run, can give representatives "greater impetus to do legislative work, and can thus expand both expertise and activity."

Aside from these changes, two other reforms are possible that could significantly disperse power within Congress, and particularly within the House. First, Congress could employ a system of alternating committee chairmen in which the chairmanship of a committee would go in one Congress to the senior committee member of the majority party or ruling coalition and, in the next Congress, to the legislator second in seniority; in the third Congress the chairmanship would return to the legislator with greatest seniority. While there are technical problems with this approach that would need some consideration, it would break down the continuous control that any one individual can have over a committee, and it thus would provide a potential access route for alternative policy perspectives.

A second possible reform might be a mandatory system of alternating committee membership in which no legislator could remain on one committee for a long continuous period. In such a system:

> continuous service on a committee could be limited to six years, after which a member would be required to leave the committee

for four years before returning, if he or she wished to return. Seniority could be determined on a combination of committee and House service, and a check would be built in to limit the overall turnover on a committee to one-third for any given Congress.

A rotation system of this type would have several consequences. First, it would prevent any small group of legislators, whatever their ideologies, from becoming entrenched in the same formal power positions for extended periods. Second, by diluting vested interests, Congress would find it easier to restructure itself as policy areas and problems change.

Finally, it would let each legislator acquire a wider range of experience [Ornstein 1974a, p. B-2].

After coordination and decentralization, the third problem in Congress is the existence of internal regulations that allow a well-placed minority immense veto power over legislation. The packing of particularly powerful committees produces this anomaly, and conservative control of committee chairmanships, the arbitrary power of the House Rules Committee, and the use of the filibuster in the Senate all tend to enhance the power of the minority. Many of the reforms outlined above are capable of reducing some of these procedural problems. Responsible multipartism, mandatory alternations of committee chairmen, and revolving committee membership would all make committee packing difficult, if not impossible, for a fading majority to implement. Short of these reforms, or in addition to them, others can be undertaken to streamline the legislative process.

First, Congress should consider a more simplified discharge procedure such that bills bottled up in committee for a specified time period could receive floor consideration if one-third of the House membership and one-third of the committee membership signed a discharge petition. Secondly, some alternative method for scheduling and regulating consideration of bills should be found to replace the Rules Committee in the House. Preferably such changes would be combined with (indeed, might be a product of) the formalization of congressional multipartism. In any case, once a bill is reported by a committee, it should be guaranteed floor consideration without the intervention or veto of any other committee. Finally, some resolution or reduction of the Senate filibuster problem must be found. As a symbolic measure, the protection of continuous debate in the Senate is desirable. Yet the delay it causes is often quite destructive not only to specific bills but to the public's confidence in the Congress as a legislative institution, particularly when the legislation that is obstructed has widespread House and popular support. One possible solution to this problem would be to link the cloture vote in the Senate to votes on a particular bill in the House. For example, bills receiving two-thirds (or three-fifths) support of those voting in the House might qualify for a reduced cloture threshold in the Senate (such as 55 percent of senators present and voting). While maintaining the underlying principle of minority protection, this rule change would help avoid the problems that might be generated by the highly idiosyncratic composition of the Senate in relation to particular bills in question.

A Final Note

None of the reforms put forth in this unit should be viewed as panaceas. The coming of multipartism will not guarantee an activist, autonomous Congress. Should the nation be seriously polarized, deadlock would characterize multipartism just as surely as it has often characterized the existing multifactionalism. But multipartism does bring with it many advantages not present in multifactionalism; the author believes that multipartism is, on balance, much the preferable arrangement. Similarly, the structural and procedural changes suggested for Congress are presented as improvements—not as ideal situations. It is one of the ironies of congressional history that the reforms of one generation (such as the coming of seniority) become the objects of the next generation's scorn. In the effort to dislodge entrenched power structures and adjust to new environmental pressures, such cycles are almost certain to occur and are a sign of institutional vigor and resilience.

Thus we must recognize that Congress today is at a crossroads of sorts. Its current situation is neither as bleak as some find it to be, nor as bright as others would hope. The role of Congress in policy formualtion has not been totally co-opted by the president. Policy surveillance is not an unknown phenomenon in Washington. Yet the regularity, efficiency, and comprehensiveness of both policy formulation and policy surveillance are not nearly as great as advocates of representative democracy would desire. Congress has responded in a number of creative ways to the complexity of the modern world and to the growth of presidential power. The coming of decentralization, professionalization, and internal regulation have encouraged congressional autonomy. In their wake, however, these changes have left untouched, or have reinforced, certain critical barriers to congressional activism.

The problem faced by Congress stems partially from its nature as a representative institution, a facet often overlooked by critics. In the halls of Congress walk legislators from all geographical areas and from many ethnic, economic, and social backgrounds. These individuals reflect a diverse range of perspectives on American society and politics. It is this diversity that provides the prime justification for their existence as a body of national decision-makers—and the primary hindrance in that decision-making. They are to identify the nation's problems, propose and debate solutions to the problems, enact legislation to ameliorate the problems, investigate the adequacy of the legislation and the adequacy of its implementation. Yet they are not of one mind; nor do they share the same viewpoints and priorities. As representatives of various constituencies and interests, they are in conflict from the outset.

The representative nature of Congress is a basic source of the conflict—and consequent deadlock—that often characterizes the institution. Still, conflict and deadlock are a price that must be paid sometimes if representative democracy is to persist. Those who would dramatically alter the role of Congress in our system in order to avoid that conflict and thus make Congress subservient to the executive, must face the fact that they are proposing a drastic alteration in our form of government, considerably lessening its representative and democratic aspects. Assuming that we wish to retain a representative democracy, we must be prepared to accept fluctuation in the activism of our government, particularly in the legislative branch. Precisely because Congress is a representative assembly, it will register many of the trends, conflicts, and deadlocks that characterize the nation generally. What is unacceptable, however, is institutional immobilism that is generated arbitrarily by inadequate congressional structure, procedure, or internal organization. The serious student of Congress must distinguish clearly between these two very different sources of deadlock.

The maintenance of representative democracy in America requires tolerance of the real differences among groups and interests; just as surely, representative democracy requires that constant attention be paid to the associations and structures by which popular government is conducted. The critical crossroads that Congress now faces lies just in this two-fold perspective. Will the nation and its leaders recognize the difference between that conflict that is implicit in representative democracy whatever its form and that conflict that grows up within a specific institution because of peculiar structural attributes not inherent in the institution? Should the first perspective prevail and obliterate the second —should all deadlock be attributed to the representative nature of Congress—then the chances for sustaining democratic government over the coming century are dim. There are no clear alternatives to a strong legislature that can balance executive power and provide popular input into governmental decision-making. A key to successful popular government lies, therefore, in our willingness to recognize and attack the structural and associational barriers that exist within Congress without destroying the crucial autonomy of Congress. Ironically, it is often easier to destroy an institution than it is to take those steps, however radical or unorthodox, that might save it—particularly when such action carries with it no guarantee of success. Yet this is the choice we may well face as we enter the last quarter of the twentieth century.

Glossary of Congressional Terms

Many terms are used throughout this unit that may be unfamiliar. The following glossary of congressional terms should clarify most of the terms. For a more extensive glossary, see *The Congressional Quarterly Almanac,* 1973.

Adjournment sine die: Adjournment without definitely fixing a day for reconvening; literally, "adjournment without a day." A session can continue until noon, January 3, of the following year, when a new session usually begins.

Adjournment to a certain day: Adjournment under a motion or resolution that fixes the next time of meeting. Neither house can adjourn for more than three days without the concurrence of the other. A session of Congress is not ended by adjournment to a certain day.

Amendment: Proposal of a legislator to alter the language or stipulations in a bill.

Appropriations bill: Grants the actual monies approved by the authorization bills, but not necessarily to the total permissible under the authorization bill. Normally an appropriations bill originates in the House, and is not acted on until its authorization measure is enacted. Regular appropriations are supposed to be passed before the start of the fiscal year to which they apply, but in recent years this has rarely happened.

Authorization bill: Authorizes a program, specifies its general aim and conduct, and unless "open-ended," puts a ceiling on monies that can be used to finance it. Usually enacted before appropriations bill is passed.

Cloture: The process by which debate can be limited in the Senate, other than by unanimous consent. A motion for cloture can apply to any measure before the Senate, including a proposal to change the chamber's rules. It requires sixteen senators' signatures for introduction and the votes of two-thirds of the senators present and voting. It is put to a roll-call vote one hour after the Senate meets on the second day following introduction of the motion. If voted, cloture limits each senator to one hour of debate.

Committee of the Whole: Unlike other committees of the House of Representatives, the Committee of the Whole has no fixed membership. It is comprised of any 100 or more House members who participate—on the floor of the chamber—in debating or altering legislation before the body. Such measures, however, first must have passed through the regular committees and be on the calendar.

Conference: A meeting between the representatives of the House and Senate to reconcile differences between the two houses over provisions of a bill. Members of the conference committee are appointed by the Speaker and the president of the Senate and are called "managers" for their respective chambers. A majority of the managers for each house must reach agreement on the provisions of the bill (often a compromise between the versions of the two chambers) before it can be sent up for floor action in the form of a "conference report." There it cannot be amended, and if not approved by both chambers, the bill goes back to conference. Elaborate rules govern the conduct of the conferences. All bills that are passed by House and Senate in slightly different form need not be sent to conference; either chamber may "concur" in the other's amendments.

Germane: Pertaining to the subject matter of the measure at hand.

All House amendments must be germane to the bill. The Senate requires that amendments be germane only when they are proposed to general appropriations bills, bills being considered under cloture, or, often, when proceeding under an agreement to limit debate.

Hearings: Committee sessions for hearing witnesses. At hearings on legislation, witnesses usually include specialists, government officials, and spokesmen for persons affected by the bills under study. Hearings related to special investigations bring forth a variety of witnesses. Committees sometimes use their subpoena power to summon reluctant witnesses. The public and press may attend "open" hearings, but are barred from "closed" or "executive" hearings.

Joint committee: A committee composed of a specified number of members of both House and Senate. Usually a joint committee is investigative in nature. There are a few standing joint committees, such as the Joint Committee on Atomic Energy and the Joint Economic Committee.

Law: An Act of Congress that has been signed by the president, or passed over his veto by the Congress.

Legislative day: The "day" extending from the time either house meets after an adjournment until the time it next adjourns. Because the House normally adjourns from day to day, legislative days and calendar days usually coincide. But in the Senate, a legislative day may, and frequently does, extend over several calendar days.

Lobby: A group seeking to influence the passage or defeat of legislation. Originally the term referred to persons who frequented the lobbies or corridors of legislative chambers in order to speak to lawmakers. The right to attempt to influence legislation is based on the First Amendment to the Constitution, which says that Congress shall make no law abridging the right of the people "to petition the Government for a redress of grievances."

Override a veto: If the president disapproves a bill and sends it back to Congress with his objection, Congress may override his veto by a two-thirds vote in each chamber.

Quorum: The number of members whose presence is necessary for the transaction of business. In the Senate and House, it is a majority of the membership (when there are no vacancies, this is 51 in the Senate and 218 in the House). A quorum is 100 in the

Committee of the Whole. If a point of order is made that a quorum is not present, the only business that may be conducted is either a motion to adjourn or a motion to direct the sergeant-at-arms to request the attendance of absentees.

Recess: Distinguished from adjournment in that a recess does not end a legislative day and therefore does not interfere with unfinished business. The rules in each house set forth certain matters to be taken up and disposed of at the beginning of each legislative day. The House, which operates under much stricter rules than the Senate, usually adjourns from day to day. The Senate often recesses.

Rider: A provision, usually not germane, tacked on to a bill that its sponsor hopes to get through more easily by including it in other legislation. Riders become law if the bills embodying them do.

Rule: The term has two specific congressional meanings. A rule may be a standing order governing the conduct of House or Senate business and listed in the chamber's book of rules. The rules deal with duties of officers, order of business, admission to the floor, voting procedures, and so on.

In the House, a rule also may be a decision made by its Rules Committee about the handling of a particular bill on the floor. The committee may determine under which standing rule a bill shall be considered, or it may provide a "special rule" in the form of a resolution. If the resolution is adopted by the House, the temporary rule becomes as valid as any standing rule, and lapses only after action has been completed to which it pertains.

A special rule sets the time limit on general debate. It may also waive points of order and even forbid all amendments except, in some cases, those proposed by the legislative committee that handles the bill. In this instance it is known as a "closed" or "gag" rule, as opposed to an "open" rule, which puts no limitation on floor action, thus leaving the bill open to alteration.

Select, or special, committee: A committee set up for a special purpose and a limited time by resolution of either House or Senate. Most special committees are investigative in nature.

Standing committee: A group permanently provided for by House or Senate rules. The standing committees at present are specified by the Legislative Reorganization Act of 1946, which broadly defines their respective jurisdictions.

Veto: Disapproval by the president of a bill or joint resolution, other than one proposing an amendment to the Constitution. When Congress is in session, the president must veto a bill within ten days, excluding Sundays, after he has received it; otherwise it becomes law with or without his signature. When the president vetoes a bill, he returns it to the house of its origin with a message stating his objections. The veto then becomes a question of high privilege. When Congress has adjourned, the president may pocket veto a bill by failing to sign it.

Bibliography

American Political Science Association, Committee on Political Parties, *Toward a More Responsible Two-Party System*. Rinehart, 1950. This is the classic argument for responsible two-partism in America.

Herbert Asher, "The Learning of Legislative Norms." *American Political Science Review*, 1973, 67:501.

Raymond A. Bauer, Ithiel de Sola Pool, and Lewis A. Dexter, *American Business and Public Policy*. Atherton, 1963. A case study of the policy-making process, illustrating vividly the interrelations between Congress and lobbyists.

Roderick Bell and David Edwards, *American Government: The Facts Reorganized*. General Learning Press, 1974.

John F. Bibby, *Legislative Oversight of Administration: A Case Study of a Congressional Committee*. Doctoral dissertation, University of Wisconsin, 1963.

Jean Blondel, *Comparative Legislatures*. Prentice-Hall, 1973. A comprehensive overview of modern legislatures throughout the world.

Charles S. Bullock III, "Committee Transfers in the United States House of Representatives." *Journal of Politics*, 1973, 35:85–117.

James Macgregor Burns, *The Deadlock of Democracy*. Prentice-Hall, 1963. A major critique of the existing American party system.

Lawrence H. Chamberlain, *The President, Congress and Legislation*. Columbia University Press, 1946. A comprehensive analysis of the relative impact of Congress and the president on the initiation and formulation of legislation, covering the late nineteenth century and the first four decades of the twentieth century.

Aage Clausen, *How Congressmen Decide: A Policy Focus.* St. Martin's Press, 1973. A quantitative analysis of legislative voting by selected dimensions during the postwar years.

Congressional Quarterly Almanac. Published yearly by the Congressional Quarterly, Inc. An excellent summary of the events of the year in Congress. Contains all roll-call votes, committee assignments, descriptions of action taken on major bills, and so on.

Joseph Cooper and David Brady, "Organization Theory and Congressional Structure." A paper presented at the Annual Meeting of the American Political Science Association, New Orleans, Louisiana, September 4–8, 1973.

Bernard Crick, *The Reform of Parliament.* Constable, 1967. An analysis of the British Parliament.

Milton C. Cummings, Jr., *Congressmen and the Electorate.* The Free Press, 1966.

Roger Davidson, *The Role of the Congressman.* Pegasus, 1969. An analysis of the attitudes of representatives based on 118 members of the Eighty-eighth Congress.

Roger H. Davidson, David M. Kovenock, and Michael K. O'Leary, *Congress in Crisis: Politics and Congressional Reform.* Wadsworth, 1969.

Marshall E. Dimock, *Congressional Investigating Committee.* Johns Hopkins Press, 1929. A classic study of congressional surveillance procedures in the nineteenth and early twentieth century.

Lawrence C. Dodd, "Committee Integration in the Senate." *Journal of Politics,* 1972, 34:1136.

Lawrence C. Dodd, "Party Coalitions in Multiparty Parliament." *American Political Science Review,* September 1974.

Lawrence C. Dodd, *Party Coalitions and Parliamentary Government.* Princeton University Press, 1975.

Lawrence C. Dodd and John C. Pierce, "The Measurement of Committee Cohesion." *Polity,* Spring, 1975.

John Donovan, *The Policy Makers.* Pegasus, 1970.

Richard F. Fenno, *The Power of the Purse.* Little, Brown, 1966. A comprehensive study of the House and Senate Appropriations Committees.

Richard F. Fenno, *Congressmen in Committees.* Little, Brown, 1973.

An excellent study of the interrelations between legislators' goals and their committee behavior.

Mark F. Ferber, "The Formation of the Democratic Study Group." In Nelson W. Polsby, ed., *Congressional Behavior*. Random House, 1971.

Louis Fisher, *President and Congress*. The Free Press, 1972. An excellent discussion of the legal and historical context of presidential-congressional relations.

Lewis A. Froman, Jr., *Congressmen and their Constituencies*. Rand McNally, 1963.

Lewis A. Froman, Jr., *The Congressional Process: Strategies, Rules, and Procedures*. Little, Brown, 1967.

George B. Galloway, *History of the House of Representatives*. Thomas Y. Crowell, 1961.

Louis C. Gawthorp, "Changing Membership Patterns in House Committee Assignments." *American Political Science Review*, 1966, 60: 366–373.

George Goodwin, Jr., "Subcommittees: Miniature Legislatures of Congress." In Leroy Rieselback, ed., *The Congressional System*. Wadsworth, 1970.

Joseph P. Harris, *Congressional Control of Administration*. The Brookings Institution, 1964. The most comprehensive modern study of congressional oversight procedures.

Ralph K. Huitt and Robert L. Peabody, *Congress: Two Decades of Analysis*. Harper & Row, 1969. Contains a comprehensive discussion by Peabody of the trends in congressional research as well as a collection of seminal articles on Congress by Ralph Huitt.

Samuel P. Huntington, "Congressional Responses to the Twentieth Century." In David B. Truman, ed., *The Congress and America's Future*. Prentice-Hall, 1965.

Sam Kernell, "Is the Senate More Liberal than the House?" *The Journal of Politics*, 1973, 35:362.

James R. Kerr, *Congressmen as Overseers: Surveillance of the Space Program*. Doctoral dissertation, Stanford University, 1963.

John Kingdon, *Congressmen's Voting Decisions*. Harper & Row, 1973. An analysis of how congressmen make their decisions when voting in the House of Representatives.

Kenneth Kofmehl, *Professional Staffs of Congress*. Purdue University Press, 1962. The most extensive description of the congressional staff system.

Warren Lee Kostroski, "Party and Incumbency in Postwar Senate Elections." *American Political Science Review*, 1973, 67:1213.

John F. Manley, *The Politics of Finance*. Little, Brown, 1964. A sequel to Fenno's analysis of the House and Senate Appropriations Committees, focusing on the Ways and Means Committee.

John F. Manley, "Wilbur Mills: A Study of Congressional Influence." *American Political Science Review*, 1969, 62:445.

Joel Margolis, "The Conservative Coalition in the United States Senate, 1933–1968." Paper presented at the Annual Meeting of the American Political Science Association, September 1972.

Nicholas Masters, "House Committee Assignments." In Leroy Rieselbach, ed., *The Congressional System*. Wadsworth, 1970.

Donald R. Matthews, *U.S. Senators and Their World*. Vintage Books, 1960. The seminal work on the Senate during the postwar years.

Donald R. Matthews and James A. Stimson, "Decision-making by U.S. Representatives: A Preliminary Model." In S. Sidney Ulmer, ed., *Political Decision-Making*. Van Nostrand, 1970.

Donald R. Matthews and James A. Stimson, *Yeas and Nays: Normal Decision-making in the House of Representatives*. Wiley-Interscience, 1975.

David R. Mayhew, *Party Loyalty Among Congressmen: The Difference Between Democrats and Republicans*. Harvard University Press, 1966. An analysis of the contrasting voting patterns that characterize congressmen in the two parties.

Lester W. Milbrath, *The Washington Lobbyists*. Rand McNally, 1963. One of the leading studies of interest groups, including a significant discussion of legislator-lobbyists relations.

Warren Miller and Donald Stokes, "Constituency Influence in Congress." *American Political Science Review*, 1963, 57: 45–57.

Ronald C. Moe and Steven C. Teel, "Congress as Policy-Maker: A Necessary Reappraisal." In Ronald C. Moe, ed., *Congress and the President*. Goodyear, 1971. An excellent extension of Lawrence Chamberlain's work for the postwar years.

William L. Morrow, *Congressional Committees*. Scribner's, 1969.

Helmut Norpoth, *Party Cohesion in the House of Representatives*. Doctoral dissertation, University of Michigan, 1974.

Norman J. Ornstein, "Causes and Consequences of Congressional Change: Subcommittee Reforms in the House of Representatives, 1970–1973." Paper presented at the Annual Meeting of the American Political Science Association, September 1973.

Norman J. Ornstein, "Committees: The Case for Rotation." *The Washington Post*, January 6, 1974a, B-2.

Norman J. Ornstein, "Legislative Behavior and Legislative Structure." Paper presented at the Seminar on Mathematical Models of Congress, Aspen, Colorado, June 1974b.

Samuel C. Patterson, "Congressional Committee Professional Staffing: Capabilities and Constraints." In Allan Kornberg and Lloyd D. Musolf, eds., *Legislatures in Development Perspective*. Duke University Press, 1970.

Robert L. Peabody, ed., *Education of a Congressman: The Newsletters of Morris K. Udall*. Bobbs-Merrill, 1972. A selected compilation of a representative's newsletters to constituents throughout the 1960s.

Robert L. Peabody, Jeffrey M. Berry, William G. Frasure, and Jerry Goldman, *To Enact a Law: Congress and Campaign Finances*. Praeger, 1972. A study of the passage of the Political Broadcast Act of 1970, later vetoed by President Nixon.

Nelson Polsby, "The Institutionalization of the House of Representatives." *American Political Science Review*, March 1968, 62:144–169.

Jeffrey Pressman, *House vs Senate*. Yale University Press, 1966.

David E. Price, *Who Makes the Law?* Schenkman, 1972.

Emmette Redford, "A Case Study of Congressional Activity: Civil Aviation, 1957–1958." *Journal of Politics*, 1960, 22:225.

George Reedy, *The Twilight of the Presidency*. New American Library, 1970. A significant discussion of American politics by a former aide to President Lyndon Johnson, suggesting provocative interpretations and reforms of the current political system.

Donald Riegle, *O Congress*. Popular Library, 1972. A representative's diary.

Leroy Rieselbach, *Congressional Politics*. McGraw-Hill, 1973. A comprehensive text on Congress.

Randall Ripley, "The Party Whip Organization in the U.S. House of Representatives." *American Political Science Review*, 1964, 58:561–576.

Randall Ripley, *Party Leaders in the House of Representatives*. Brookings Institution, 1967.

Randall Ripley, *Majority Party Leadership in Congress*. Little, Brown, 1969a.

Randall Ripley, *Power in the Senate*. St. Martin's Press, 1969b.

John S. Saloma III, *Congress and the New Politics*. Little, Brown, 1969.

Malcolm Shaw and John D. Lees, "Committees in Legislature and the Political System." Paper presented at the Ninth World Congress of The International Political Science Association, August 1973.

George Shipley, *Congress and the Agencies.* Dissertation in progress, University of Texas, 1974.

John E. Sinclair, "Legislators and Lobbyists in Canada and the United States: The Impact of Institutions on Individual Behavior." Paper prepared for presentation at the Annual Meeting of the Association for Canadian Study in the U.S., Austin, Texas, March 1974.

Arthur G. Stevens, Jr., *Informal Groups and Decision-Making in the House of Representatives.* Doctoral dissertation, The University of Michigan, 1971.

James Sundquist, *Politics and Policy.* The Brookings Institution, 1968. A major study of the origin and fate of legislation during the Eisenhower, Kennedy, and Johnson years.

Donald G. Tacheron and Morris K. Udall, *The Job of Congressman.* Bobbs-Merrill, 1970.

Julius Turner and E. V. Schneier, *Party and Constituency.* Johns Hopkins University Press, 1970. An updating of the classic study of congressional roll-call voting.

David J. Vogler, *The Third House: Conference Committees in the U.S. Congress.* Northwestern University Press, 1971. The most comprehensive study of conference committees.

Aaron Wildavsky, *The Politics of the Budgetary Process.* Little, Brown, 1964. A dated but excellent description of the budgetary process, placing the role of Congress in perspective.

Woodrow Wilson, *Congressional Government.* Meridian Books, 1965. First published in 1885, this is a classic study of Congress by its most famous student.

Raymond E. Wolfinger and Joan Heifitz Hollinger, "Safe Seats, Seniority, and Power in Congress." In Leroy Rieselbach, ed., *The Congressional System.* Wadsworth, 1970.